Also by Dr. Oseno Ben

1.

*County Governments' Guide Book on
Financial Management.*

2.

*Alternative Financing Models for
Saccos in Kenya.*

3.

*Internal Control System: Perspective
of Saccos in Kenya.*

4.

*The Conceptual Framework:
Conceptualization in Research Proposal,
Project and Thesis.*

OSENO BEN

RESEARCH ENTERPRISE

TOPIC AND CONCEPTUAL FRAMEWORK

RESEARCH ENTERPRISE
TOPIC AND CONCEPTUAL FRAMEWORK

First Published 2019

Layout and design by R D Okang'a Ooko
Typeset in Nairobi by Oba Kunta Octopus

Printed and Published in Kenya by:
Oba Kunta Octopus
P.O. Box   100240 - 00101 Nairobi
Tel: 0722 493 896

ISBN 978 9966 132 45 1

For further information regarding special discounts for bulk purchases, please contact Dr. Oseno Ben Special Sales at +254720053915 email address: osenoben@yahoo.com

This book is dedicated to my mother for instilling a sense of responsibility in us as we grew up and her continued concern in every development in our lives.

PREFACE

When a reader goes through a research topic, its expected that the study issue should be reflected with no ambiguity. However, this may not be the case in some studies. A casual survey of research projects and theses in the shelves of our institutions reveal serious research topic design weakness.

In addition, designing a conceptual framework with the relevant study variables, their constructs or measurements precisely prescribed is proving to be a very complex issue. Further, aligning the study objectives with the conceptual framework variables in making a study topic coherent to the framework is quite a challenge.

This book is interested in bridging these gaps by presenting a thorough understanding of how a research topic should be stated and the development of a conceptual framework in the social science research.

FOREWARD

This brief but potent book; "Research Enterprise: Topic and Conceptual Framework" is a significant contribution by the author to the idea of "a research enterprise."

The author employs simple direct language in exposing otherwise what initially sounds as complex to a student engaging in a research activity; the research topic; the conceptual framework in relation to literature revenue, objectives, hypotheses and/or research questions.

This book is likely to be very useful to students beginning to engage in a research enterprise at certificate, diploma and degree levels.

Prof. Frank K. Matanga
Professor of Political Science
Peace & Conflict Studies Department
School of Disaster Management & Humanitarian Assistance
Masinde Muliro University of Science & Technology

19th May, 2019

Acknowledgements

I wish to appreciate my fellow lecturers and other researchers for their opinion and suggestions in making this great piece of work a success. To my family, I sincerely thank you for the moral support and providing a warm domestic environment which enabled the production of this book. I also would like to thank my publisher for having faith in my work and working round the clock to ensure that we present a quality work.

Users of the book

This book can be used by diploma students, undergraduate and postgraduate students. Instructors and lecturers may also find the book useful in preparing instructional materials and beefing up literature in Research Methodology unit.

Key features of the book

- Use of simple and straight forward language has been carried throughout the book in order to enhance the reader's understanding.

- Division of the book in different chapters with each section carrying a particular theme.

- In each chapter, there is an abstract summarizing the content of the chapter to prepare the reader on what is expected in each chapter.

Scope of the book

The book provides a comprehensive coverage of how to design a research topic and how a conceptual framework should be developed. Challenges students face in developing their research topics and how to overcome such challenges as well as designing a conceptual framework

How to use the book effectively

The author advises the readers to systematically go through the ten chapters of the book to built flow of themes covered in the book.

CONTENTS

PART ONE:
RESEARCH TOPIC DESIGN

CHAPTER ONE   1
BACKGROUND TO A RESEARCH TOPIC /1

CHAPTER TWO   8
CONCEPTUALIZING A RESEARCH TOPIC /8

PART TWO:
CONCEPTUAL FRAMEWORK

CHAPTER FIVE /40
CONCEPTUAL FRAMEWORK VARIABLES / 40

CHAPTER SIX / 55
FORMS OF CONCEPTUAL FRAMEWORK / 55

CHAPTER SEVEN   / 68
CONCEPTUAL FRAMEWORK AND RESEARCH OBJECTIVES / 68

CHAPTER TEN / 99
CONCEPTUAL FRAMEWORK AND LITERATURE REVIEW /99

BIBLIOGRAPHY / 108

LIST OF FIGURES

PART ONE:

RESEARCH TOPIC DESIGN

Chapter One

BACKGROUND TO A RESEARCH TOPIC

Abstract

Designing a research topic is a critical aspect in research proposal writing because it is from a study title that enables a reader to figure out at a glance the issue a researcher would like to scientifically investigate. A research topic is a short statement containing the variables of a study and the study site where a study will be conducted. In some cases, the research design is carried on a study title. A good research topic should be precise and clear since the research problem, study objectives as well as conceptual framework development stem from the study topic. There are different approaches which can be adopted when designing a research topic such as interrogative and passive approaches to a research topic development. Therefore, background to a research topic design introduces us to the meaning of a research topic development, components of a research topic, qualities of a good research topic as well as the approaches adopted when designing a research topic.

Key words:
Background and Research topic design.

Introduction
This chapter presents the meaning and the components of a research topic as well as research topic design approaches.

Meaning of a research topic

A research topic/title is a short statement containing the variables that a researcher is interested in investigating as well as the study site. The variables constituting study topic/title are independent and dependent variables. However, in some cases, even the intervening and moderating variables are also presented in a study topic/title.

When designing a study topic/title, the reader of your research should be able to extract meaning out of the topic/title at a glance since the key variables to your study are explicitly detailed in the topic/title. Besides the variables, the study site is a key component in a study topic/title because it shows the organization, country, county, continent, community, region, sector or institution where the study is to be conducted. This gives the reader the opportunity to connect the study variables with the unique aspect of the organization or country the study is premised and whether the variables under investigation are justified to be researched in such an organization or country.

A study topic/title is a one sentence summary of the statement of the research problem, scope of the study itself and in some cases the research design. Just as it is said that, the first impression always last, a study topic/title gives the impression of what a study is. In view of the foregoing, it is vital to note that the design of a study topic/title should be precise and clear since it depict a phenomenon under investigation and where the investigation is to be conducted.

In the structure of a research paper, a study title occupies a special position by appearing first followed by an abstract then the introduction. The body which occupies the largest portion then follows, as conclusion and recommendations take the last sections respectively. This structure is illustrated in figure 1.1;

Figure 1.1: Structure of a research paper

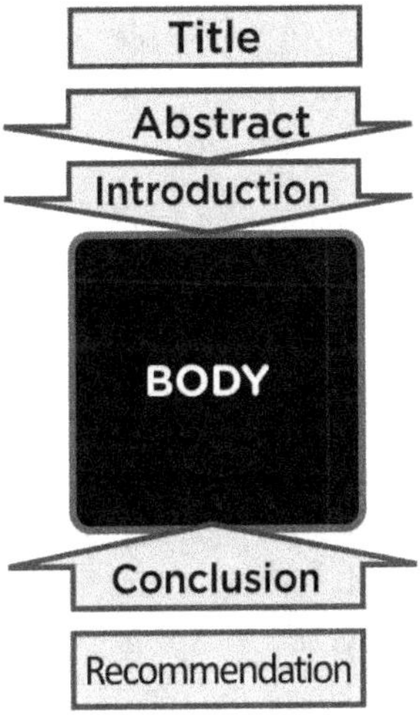

Source: Oseno (2019)

Components of a research topic/title

The components of a research topic/title are:

> i)   *Study variables*
>
> ii) *Study site*
>
> iii) *Research design*

i) Study variables

The most important thing to note on the study variables in a study topic/title is the status of the variables. What do I mean by the status? Status of a variable means its role in terms of whether it is the influencer variable or the influenced or intervening (stepping stone) variable or it is simply a moderator. The status of the influencer variable and the influenced variable are the most critical in a study topic/title. The absences of any of those two variables in a study topic/title makes it incomplete or when the two are confused by a researcher in her study topic/title, the entire study logic and flow may be lost.

ii) Study site

A study site just as had been explain in the meaning of the research topic/title section simply means where the study is to be located. A study can be located in a country, a county, an organization, a sector, a region, a continent among others. The study location should match the variables or the phenomenon to be investigated and at the justification sub-section in a study, the researcher must logically present a convincing argument as to why the study location was chosen. Reasons justifying choice of a particular study location may be in the form of demographic factors, prevalence, minimal studies and even inconsistencies in the previous study findings among other reasons.

iii) Research design

Research design is the approach a researcher will adopt in conducting a study. A case study research design is commonly carried in many study topics/titles where the researcher is interested in having an in-depth study of the study location. Also it allows the researcher to concentrate the research resources in a particular study site as well as when the organizations of interest exhibit similar characteristics and the study of a few of them can make the findings scientifically generalized on the others. Evaluative studies as well as cross sectional studies also feature in study topics/titles.

Qualities of a Good Research Topic/Title

A good research topic/title should have the following characteristics:

i) Should be precise and clear

ii) Should capture at least the independent and dependent variables

iii) Should be interrogative or descriptive or declarative or compounded

iv) It should contain the study location

v) The words should not be more than eighteen

vi) The variables should match the study premises.

Research Topic/Title Design Approaches

Researchers do adopt different approaches when designing their research topics/titles as long as they meet the requirements of qualities of a good research topic/title. Institutions of higher learning have also aided the development of research topics/titles by providing varied guidelines on how the topics/titles of studies are to be formulated more especially for the post-graduate students. In some institutions, the use of such terms as "effect", "impact", "an investigation of" or "an evaluation of", or "an analysis of" are discouraged while other institutions have embraced them.

The institutions that are against the use of such terms cite monotony of the words and that such terms are better used when writing diploma projects or undergraduate projects, while the advocates of the usage of such terms argue that they make a research topic/title interrogative and the postulated course-effect relationship between the study variables can be easily extracted. Besides, the connectivity of the variables under investigation becomes apparent in a study topic/title. In spite of the varied schools of thought, the following approached can be adopted when designing a research topic/title:

i) Interrogative approach
ii) Passive approach

i) Interrogative approach emphasis the use of certain words on a study topic/title such as effect of or impact of or an investigation of or an evaluation of or an analysis of or comparative examination of one aspect on another. This approach has been widely used in many studies and it seems to be the order of the day, no wonder those who are against the approach argue that it is monotonous.

ii) Passive approach commonly use the connector word "and" to connect the independent variable to the dependent variable. For example, we can have a topic/title stated as "customer satisfaction and sales volume of the Uniliver Company products in East Africa, "disaster risk financing and risk reduction in the Kenyan national disaster platform" or "teacher-pupil ratio and learner performance in the public primary schools in the coastal region of Kenya". The passive approach elicits some thinking in the mind of the reader in respect to what could be the influencer variable in the topic/title and at the same time the influenced variable. This state of dilemma on some readers is the weakness to this approach of designing a study topics/title.

Specific Research Topic/Title Types

a) Descriptive

b) Declarative

c) Interrogative

d) Compounded

Chapter Two

CONCEPTUALIZING A RESEARCH TOPIC

Abstract

Conceptualizing a research topic is the process of presenting in a concrete form a researcher's own understanding of the issue being investigated in a single short sentence known as a research topic/title. Conceptualization of a research topic can be appropriately done upon a researcher undertaking an in-depth literature review of the issue being investigated. This enables the researcher to identify the inconsistencies in the previous study findings, hypothetical relationships between variables and identification of theories which may inform the study issues among other aspects. Therefore it enables a researcher to conceptualize a research topic. The choice of study variables as well as their constructs which appropriately match the study issue is of essence in conceptualizing a study topic. A well conceptualized research topic will aid the formulation of SMART study objectives, appropriate design of a conceptual framework as well as guiding preparation of data collection instruments.

Key Words

Conceptualizing and Research topic.

Introduction

The chapter details the meaning of conceptualization, conceptualized variables, variable constructs and measures as well as the basis of constructs and measurements assignment. Also the chapter covers factors to consider when assigning constructs and measurements to a variable.

Meaning of Conceptual Framework

Having gone through literature, made observations, listened to arguments of others on an issue, experienced certain phenomenon, identified inconsistencies in study findings as well as emerging dynamics in the society be they inform of practices, policies, laws or regulations, technological, demographic, competitive, scientific among others, a researcher can present her concrete thinking or reflection in a short single statement know as a study topic/title. That state of reflection is called conceptualization. The perception of the researcher should be guided by the above mentioned aspects to sustain logic and flow in a study topic/title as well as the research problem.

The logic in the study variables conceptualized is critical when designing a study title because it forms the tenets of the study phenomenon. It is not easy to get it right for many students more especially when they are commencing their proposal writing. However, the solution to that challenge is literature review, engaging the experts and understanding the organization or sector you want to use as a study location.

Literature review will enrich you with knowledge over the phenomenon, you will be able to distinguish symptoms of a problem from the main issue and peripheral issues from the cracks of the matter. Get to know what other researchers did, variables they studied, methodological approaches adopted and their findings. Nature of the study site, its unique characteristics which puts it apart from others in the same sector or industry should be well understood by the researcher. General literature review is vital too at this time. The idea of students writing anything they imagine of as a topic/title to a study without a deep reflection as informed by literature review on the logic and flow is not appropriate and this has led to weak studies and students getting frustrated during the proposal defense or even at the concept note presentation stage. They leave the panel confused and worse than they came. They end up bad mouthing the department, panelists and the institution by extension as frustrating their effort towards their career progression.

Conceptualized variables

It is vital to know the variables you are conceptualizing because you may end up confusing those variables in your study topic/title as well as the entire study. The distinction between the independent variable and the dependent variable is necessary. The independent variable is also known as the influencer variable. When this variable is manipulated, it may influence another variable such as dependent variable. The dependent variable is the influenced variable and the influence necessitated may be measured by a range of or just a single indicator in respect to how the study is scoped.

Intervening and moderating variables need also to be distinguished by the researcher when conceptualizing the variables. An intervening variable lies between the independent and dependent variables. It is the bridge variable, a stepping stone variable which is influenced by the influencer variable and the output of that influence on the intervening variable resultantly influence the dependent variable.

For example, in a study titled "effect of marketing strategies on customer satisfaction and organizational performance: A case of East African Breweries limited Company" or "impact of public financial management on financial distress and the operations of the county governments in Kenya" or "control activities and control environment on the performance of internal control system in the parastatals in Kenya".

The intervening variables in the suggested research topics/titles are customer satisfaction, financial distress and control environment respectively. When conceptualizing the intervening variable the most important thing to take into account is the centrality of the variable on the phenomenon being investigated. It minimizes "far fetching" and forcing illogical conceptual connection or association between the independent and dependent variables.

The moderating variable is rather passive in conceptualization as compared to the intervening variable because of the moderation effect it has on the dependent variable at the intersection point between the independent and dependent variables as usually shown by an arrow in the conceptual framework. The constructs of these variables should be picked carefully in respect to where the study is located as well as the uniqueness to the study and their number should be controlled that is just a few key ones to be identified.

Antecedent variable causes influence on the independent variable and because of the resultant influence, the independent variable will influence the dependent variable.

There are certain conditions to be met in classifying a variable as an antecedent variable. These are:

i) The variable must be related in some logical sense to the other variables more especially the independent variable.

ii) When the antecedent variable is controlled, the relationship between the independent and the dependent variables should not disappear rather it could be enhanced or reduced.

iii) When the independent variable is controlled or its influence removed, there should not be any relationship between the antecedent variable and dependent variable.

Course effect relationship can be used to explain the antecedent variable. In conceptualizing variables to a study, the researcher can start by examining theories in establishing cause effect description of a phenomenon which can consequently lead to other effects. It is like the multiplier effect of inflation on the economy or the famous vicious cycle of poverty; "if there is low savings, investments will be low and with low investments, production will reduce and with reduction in production, income will be low and this will lead to low savings. In this case, low savings antecedate on the investments and the resultant influence affect production and the sequence can continue over and over again.

Variable constructs and measurements

Variable constructs are the components of a variable. A human body is made up of different parts such as the head, legs or reproductive organs among others. Motivation can be synchronized to a human body and the components of motivation may be in the forms of; monetary reward, material reward, recognization (verbal, certificate award), working condition as well as management style.

The constructs of a variable thus is often confused by many with the variable itself. These constructs help the researcher to formulate the study objectives. Variable measurements is a term usually used when dependent variable is being examined. We previously noted that the influencer variable influences the dependent variable. But the question is; how do you measure the influence necessitated by the influencer variable on the influenced variable?

The influence may be measured by appropriate indicators of the influenced variable. For example, in a hypothetical topic/title; "motivation and employee productivity in the cement manufacturing firms in Kenya", the influenced variable is employee productivity. The measurements of the variable may be; number of units/output, number of spoilt units in a given quantity, quality of finished product among others.

Basis of constructs and measures assignment

Assignment of constructs to a variable as well as identification of measurements to a variable is often challenging. Thus the guiding criteria on how to do this is very vital and a research study with appropriate constructs and measurements is worth the time and the resources invested in the study.

The following aspects form the basis upon which constructs and measures of variables are assigned:

a) Practices
b) Laws and regulations
c) Policies
d) Nature and characteristics of objects
e) Trends and dynamics in the market
f) Strategies

g) Techniques, approaches or methods
h) Principles and standards
i) Findings from previous studies
j) Recommendations of previous studies
k) Types or forms of different aspects such as management style, traditions etc
l) Society concerns such as leakage of national examinations as well as quality of education in the universities in Kenya.
m) Theories
n) Cultural practices and beliefs
o) Schools of thought/divergence opinion.
p) Orientations
q) Constitutional provisions
r) Structures such as organization structures or market structures
s) Emerging issues
t) Business cycles
u) Continents, regions, countries, counties or sub-counties or villages unique demographics, economic activities, ecological forces etc
v) Race, tribe or sub-tribes
w) Political competition
x) Religious doctrines
y) Sex, language, population, age etc

Although the listed aspects of guiding assignment of variable constructs and measurements may not be exhaustive, they form appropriate guide for a student developing a study topic and a whole proposal in the social science research.

Factors to consider when assigning constructs and measurements to a variable

When a researcher is identifying the contracts and measurements to a study variable he should take into account certain factors. These factors are as follows:

a) Study site or location. If they are practices, as constructs to a certain variable under investigation, are they exercised in that industry, sector or organization? You must ensure you marry the practices to the study site or location.

b) Expected outcome. If the independent variable constructs are manipulated. This will enable the researcher to assign appropriate measures to the dependent variable. For example, Sacco growth measurements.

c) Hierarchy of the constructs as may be contextualized by the researcher as informed by prevalence, dominance, status in the phenomenon among other considerations. It is important to note that not all constructs relating to a variable and considering the study site can be investigated in a study. Thus a researcher picks-on the core other than the "peripheral" constructs or "immaterial constructs that may make the study weak. Although further studies may be carried on them to establish their position in the phenomenon of interest by other researchers.

d) Fulcrum of constructs. At times students list a number of constructs of the independent variable and the list can be long. Under such cases the number of objectives to be investigated become so many and even non SMART, more especially being specific and measurable qualifications.

The solution to this is identification of a common denominator or fulcrum such as teacher factors, pupil centred factors, school based factors and other stakeholders factor. If a study was to investigate "determinants of learner performance in the public primary school among the pastoralist communities in Kenya", one may be tempted to list a number of determinants such as; Insecurity, cultural practices, syllabus coverage, teacher commitment, pupil nutrition, community attitude towards education, home to school distance, learning and teaching materials, teacher-student ratio, pupil entry behavior, age of pupils on admission to school, community economic status, opinion on girl pupil or teacher quality.

These factors can be grouped into the four major categories called denominator or fulcrum constructs as demonstrated below:

i) Teacher factors
- Syllabus coverage
- Teacher commitment
- Teacher quality

ii) School based factors
- Home to school distance
- Learning and teaching materials
- Teacher-pupil ratio

iii) Pupil centred factors
- Pupil nutrition
- Entry behavior
- Age of pupil on admission

iv) **Other stakeholders factor**

- Infrastructure - government
- Cultural practices – community
- Attitude of community towards education – community
- Community economic status – government

The common denominator makes the factors to be reduced to four and these will form the objectives of the study:

a) Inter-relationship between or among the constructs can be looked into if any. This depends on what the researcher may be interested in establishing about the phenomenon and the assumptions of the study.

b) Single or multiple measure of a construct. When an independent variable construct is manipulated, the anticipated influence on a dependent variable may be measured by one indicator or a number of indicators. Those measures should observe the nature of the phenomenon being investigated and the study site in order to assign appropriate measurements.

Chapter Three

RESEARCH TOPIC ORIGINATION

Abstract

Research topic origination refers to where a research topic derives its validity from. It involves examining literature, drawing from theories, consulting experts and scholars as well as being enlightened by the media revelations. A research topic origination can also be guided by the researcher's own experience, paying field visits, focus group discussion and academic fora such as proposal and thesis presentations or seminars and conferences. When originating a study topic, challenges are abound and among them, researcher centred challenges are critical such as inadequate knowledge of a phenomenon being investigated, choice of the study site, study scope among other challenges. These challenges can be overcome by undertaking literature review, appropriate choice of study design, scope, being familiar with the area of the study among other factors

Key Word

Research topic origination.

Introduction

The chapter documents the meaning of research topic origination, sources of research topic origination, challenges experienced by a researcher when originating a research topic as well as remedies to overcome the challenges.

Meaning of Research Topic/title Origination

Topic/title origination means where a study topic/title stems from. It further means the birth place of a study topic/title under investigation. When a researcher wants to come up with a research problem, there are certain things that help the researcher in developing a research problem. Such things are theories, literature review, media, one's personal experience, seeking guidance from experienced researchers or scholars or visiting sites aid the researcher in developing a research problem, as well as topic origination.

A research topic/title is just but a one-off sentence summary of a research problem thus the guiding factors on how to generate a research problem similarly help in the origination of a study topic/title. A well thought out study topic/title is closely associated with the research problem a study would like to investigate and a poorly designed study topic/title makes it hard to extract meaning out of it thus the study problem may not be clear.

Where a topic/title originates from

Topic/title origination is from the following sources:

a) Existing theories
b) Existing literature
c) Media revelations
d) Site/field visits
e) Discussion with experts
f) Academic proposal and thesis presentations or seminars and conferences.
g) One's own experience
h) Replication of previous studies

These sources aiding the origination of a study topic/title are presented as follows according to Abel M. Gitau in his book title *"Qualitative Research Methods";-*

a) Existing theories

An existing theory in an academic or professional field is a good source of a research problem. A theory contains generalizations and hypothesized relationships among and between variables and concepts that can be scientifically tested. Such tests can be done through the research process. Alternatively, a researcher can choose to focus on some aspects of a theoretical system or conceptual schemes which have been development by others. This leads to validation or otherwise of existing generalizations within the theoretical principles. This is quite common with studies that are theory based. However, there are many studies that are not necessarily theory based.

b) Existing literature

A systematic reading programme in the general area of interest is perhaps the best way of locating specific research problems. Journal papers and dissertations, research reports, textbooks and other literature that focus on the subject the student is interested in studying are perhaps the most helpful sources when trying to identify a research problem. By referring to these documents, the researcher gains a good background of basic information and an insight into various issues that could be studied in specific areas of interest. Most journal papers and theses, for example, state categorically further areas of research as part of their recommendations. Consequently this will help the researcher to originate appropriate research topic.

c) Media revelations

With the rapid growth of information technology, the media has become a rich source of information in many countries. The internet, radio, television, newspapers, journals etc relay a great deal of information to millions of people every day. Issues which are frequently reported in the media often drive the research agenda. Researchable problems can therefore be identified from the myriad of issues reported daily by the media.

It is however important to note that, although a certain issue may not be critically important, the media may sensationalize it in order to attract attention and make profit by selling more copies. Media reports may also contain a great deal of speculations, personal and propaganda. Such reports therefore lack the scientific rigour, which is a necessary and distinctive characteristic of disciplined inquiry.

Students who source their research problems from the media should therefore be cautious because some of the reports appearing in the media about issues may tend to be subjective and speculative with the aim of fulfilling a particular political agenda or promoting biased views. However, experienced researchers are often able to separate the wheat from the chaff when they rely on media reports to inform their research.

d) Site/field visits

Researchers are always looking for new grounds to break in order to expand their horizons fields of knowledge. For beginning researchers, new events and occurrences that happen in particular geographical areas should attract their attention and inspire them to conduct in-depth research to understand such phenomena. Site visits to areas where certain events occur is perhaps one of the best strategies of identifying critical areas to research on. For example, a volcanic eruption may occur and spill hot, molten lava, ash and dangerous gases. These elements often have disastrous public health effects on populations. A visit to such a site would help the researcher generate various researchable topics in order to understand the effects of such an event on the human population, animals, plants and the physical environment.

As stated already, serious researchers often make visits to sites where unusual events have happened so that they can identify areas of immediate research. Similarly, students who may be interested in research on issues such as insecurity, floods, epidemics, drought or parcels of land disputed by ethnic groups, should ideally make visits and observe first-hand the contexts of the events that they are interested in investigating.

These site visits help researchers observe and critically think about what should be the priority issues to study and how the research problem should be formulated. It is disheartening to note that much of the research conducted in Africa is being funded and undertaken by foreigners. Foreign researchers are often the first to arrive on the scene when an unusual event occurs in an African Country. They collect the data, analyze it, we hardly get to know or use the results. This should be a challenge to local researchers, professionals and academicians. Local researchers should be motivated to investigate local problems that face local populations.

e) Discussion with experts

Discussing topics in a particular area of interest with colleagues during lectures, seminars, informal gatherings etc, helps students locate current topics in their fields of interest that they might want to research on. Brainstorming with other researchers, teachers, professionals in the field or interest and colleagues helps the student to organize his or her thoughts more logically and to mentally visualize the topic clearly before stating it in words.

f) Academic proposal and thesis presentation or seminars and conferences

Students, professionals and scholars gain invaluable experience and insight by attending local and international conferences. It is in such conferences where suggestions on areas that need further research in a particular field are debated. Availability of funds for specific areas may often be announced in such conferences. The student also gets to interact with the "community of practice" in research: This is a group of scholars, practitioners and researchers in a given field who respond to and communicate to each other through published journal articles, presentations in conferences, e-mails, skype and other channels of communication. They form powerful networks that aim to strengthen research and innovation in specific subject areas.

g) One's own experience

A person's everyday experiences provide a rich source of researchable problems. First-hand observation and reflection on an intriguing experience triggers the researcher's mind, creating the desire to deeply understand the phenomenon associated with particular experience. For example, a person who has been discriminated on the basis of their colour, religious beliefs, sex or political ideology may be motivated to carry out a study in any of these areas. Even for an experienced researcher, his or her daily encounters, experiences and interactions with others and with the surrounding social and physical environments, become the most compelling sources of research topics.

h) Replication of previous studies

Replicating a study involves carrying out a research project that has been done previously. In this case, the problem and the procedures that are used in the proposed study are identical to a study that has previously been conducted by another researcher. Replication is usually done to find out whether findings hold over time and across similar or different environments, populations or geographical settings.

Challenges encountered when originating a study topic/title

Challenges are abound when originating a research study topic/title. These challenges are spurred by a number of factors making topic/title design in a study quite challenging to a number of students. The challenges limiting the origination of a study topic/title are as follows:

a) Inadequate knowledge on the issue you want to investigate. This is mainly associated with limited literature review. You need to read widely and deeply as well as between the lines about the phenomenon you want research on.

b) Study site or location

Shallow knowledge on where you are to premise your study

may make you mis or mis-match certain aspects of a study topic/title. You need to read more about the organization or the region you will conduct your study, make observation as well by paying site visits to deepen your understanding on the study site characteristics or events.

c) Scope of the study

A study scope may be too wide or narrow and this may create uncertainty on the study focus as well as researchability of the phenomenon. The scope aspects are determined by the number and nature of variables, the organization or firm you want to study, the variable constructs and the period to be covered by the study for example, from 2003 to 2016) since the introduction of free primary education in Kenya.

d) Conceptualizing challenges

Many students face challenges of conceptualizing or visualizing the issues of interest for investigation. The aspects of contextualizing the knowledge gathered from the literature review is quite challenging and this is where the input of a supervisor is critical to recast the students roaming understanding.

e) Student's biasness owing to stored knowledge on

the study site gained out of work experience or otherwise.
A student's biasness makes her fixated, rigid, and subjective in presenting a study topic. It's like a researcher who already knows the results of the study even before going to the field for data collection. While that experience is good in sharpening the students understanding of the phenomenon, caution should be exercised in drawing from it.

f) **Minimal input of a supervisor.** In certain cases, some supervisors are too busy thus they have very little time if any to look at the student's work. Besides, the competences of some of the supervisors are wanting hence the gaps in the topic/title design.

g) **Uplifting of "ready-made work" from the internet and other sources.** This is boarding on ethical concerns where students uplift projects and theses of previous researchers then they go about making some changes such as study sites, replacing factors with determinants, effect replaced with impact, etc this shows that the student does not have any grasp of what the phenomenon to be investigated, its variables and their constructs.

h) **Hurriedly conceived studies.** When students get to realize that concept notes presentation date or proposal defense date is around the corner, they hurriedly rush to craft some not-well thought out research topics. It is important to note that, it is you the researcher who is expected to have an in-depth knowledge on what you want to research on. The other parties work is simply to give guidance in terms of scope, measurement of variables, appropriateness of the research design, choice of analysis tools, appropriateness of theories if any etc.

i) **Limited consultation.** Some students strictly work with their supervisors in spite of certain gaps which may be inherent in the work. The second eye is always necessary, seek opinion from other researchers, get to know how others think about your work and information sharing has always built an otherwise weak idea.

How to overcome challenges on a research topic/ title design

The experienced challenges encountered when designing a research topic/title can be overcome by:

i) **Undertaking literature review.** Both general and empirical literature is vital for a good research topic/ title development. Critical literature review is essential, gaps can be identified in the previous studies as well as the scope of the study at hand can be delimitated appropriately.

ii) **Get to understand the scope of your study.** Avoid being too narrow or broad in your study scope. Selection of the variables and the study site or location to be studied forms the scope of your study.

iii) **Choose a study area your one familiar with.** It will enable you understand the phenomenon you are investigating well. The basics of what is required of a study area become easily understood and you can advance from the basics to more complex issues in the study area. This may pose a challenge to one who is not familiar with the study area and literature review is vital at this point.

iv) **Understanding thoroughly where you will premise your study.** If the study will be conducted in the county governments, get know what they are dealing in, policies, regulations as well as constitutional provisions governing their operations, challenges they are experiencing, administrative structures, relationship with the national government and other arms of the government among other issues.

(v) Embracing consultation with other researchers. This will open up your thinking and approach to the study. You get to learn new ideas that can add value to your work.

vi) Striking a balance between the already stored information (experience) and the tenets of your study. Don't be over carried by what you know because this may make you be biased in your approach to the study.

vii) Striving for originality and uniqueness of your work as compared to other studies in the same area. Avoid uplifting people's work, you will be less grounded on what you are doing and also it is illegal. Progressive report schemes should be adopted by institutions to monitor students work.

viii) Understanding your supervisor is very important. Get to know his view point and allow him or her to have the freedom to criticize your work. However, in a respectful and logical manner present you view point of the topic/title to your supervisor without fear. This will enable both of you to strike a balance. Also support your arguments with reliable source materials such as journals to enhance your supervisor's understanding of your point of argument.

PART TWO:

CONCEPTUAL FRAMEWORK

Chapter Four

INTRODUCTION TO CONCEPTUAL FRAMEWORK

Abstract

A conceptual framework is a diagrammatical presentation of the variables in a study. A conceptual framework presents a researchers understanding of the issue being investigated upon conducting a literature review. The diagram will indicate by use of arrows the possible relationships between the variables and their interrelationships. A conceptual framework is designed based on examination of the existing theories, empirical studies, existing policies, laws and regulations as well as business practices among others.

Key Word

Conceptual framework.

Introduction

This chapter presents, the meaning of a conceptual framework, qualities of a good conceptual framework, rationale of a conceptual framework in a study, relationships in the conceptual framework, researchers and the conceptual framework as well as the premises of the conceptual framework.

Meaning of a conceptual framework

A conceptual framework is developed to help a researcher perceived the interrelationships between the study variable. Researchers anchor their studies on existing theories, as well as models, thus such studies derive their validity from those theories or models. This means that the researcher recast the variables of a study after assessing the tenets of the theories or/ and models. However, it is vital to recognize that theories and models do not generally exist in all areas of study and specific issues that a researcher may be interested in investigating may lack a theory or a model to be premised upon. To this end, a researcher may present his perspective in a diagrammatical form demonstrating the subsisting hypothetical relationships between or among the variables. This diagrammatical illustration of the variables is referred to as self-conceptualization of a study by a researcher and that which is designed by the researcher is known as the conceptual framework.

A conceptual framework is a summary in diagrammatical manner of all the variables that a researcher is interested in investigating systematically. A conceptual framework is born out of review of the documented literature in an area of interest to the researcher. This involves digging into the past literature where the researcher examines what others did in that area of study, the scope of previous studies, the organizations or communities or countries in which the studies were conducted. Besides the periods they were done, the type of data collected, instruments used in data collection and data analysis, are to be examined by the researcher. This will helps the researcher to identity issues that might have not been adequately addressed. At the same time even if they were examined in the previous studies they might be more focused in the developed countries, or concentrated in the urban set-ups, or more oriented towards the manufacturing sector.

This manifests that the findings of such studies may be skewed in their application towards the developed countries, urban areas and the manufacturing sector. The scope of the constructs in a particular study variable or the cause-effect relationship between the variables in a study as well as the nature of correlation between the variables of a study can further be examined by the researcher. It is from the review of literature that the researcher is able to design a conceptual framework in a condensed or distilled extraction from the general perspective issues in a study to specific aspects that the researcher would like to systematical investigate in filling the existing gap in the literature.

In the literature review, the researcher examines a central idea and how other concepts relate to it. For example, employee motivation may be the central concept or idea and the other concepts that relate to it are the working conditions, employee remuneration, promotion, and job security. The central concept which is the independent variable and the other concepts are the aspects of the independent variable.

In examining the relationship between the independent and dependant variable, the researcher should not only show how the central concept and the other variables relate but also the interrelationship among the other aspects of the independent variable.

Qualities of a good conceptual framework

i) A good conceptual framework should not only outline the variables in a study with little or no indication of the possible relationships among them but also precisely show the possible relationships and interrelationships.

ii) A good conceptual framework will show how the framework affects the research design, data collection procedures and later guide the interpretation of the findings.

iii) A good conceptual framework should also help in formulating prepositions or hypotheses depicting relationships between the variables and expected outcomes of the research which can be tested later using data collected through appropriate methodology.

iv) A good conceptual framework should present all the variables with their specific aspects outlining the phenomenon under investigation.

v) A good conceptual framework should strike a balance between simplicity and complexity in presenting the variables and the hypothetical relationships between or among the variables in a study.

Conceptual frameworks vary according to levels depending on the phenomenon being studied, how the problem has been defined, the research objectives and the level of conceptualization by the researcher, that is how a researcher has understood the phenomenon.

Rationale of using a conceptual framework in a Study.

Many researchers have used conceptual frameworks in their studies because of the following reasons:

i) To enable a researcher to conceptualize the relationship between variables in the study.

ii) To help the reader to quickly see the proposed relationship in the study.

iii) A researcher puts a conceptual framework to test in order to establish the significance of the proposed relationships.

iv) A researcher may, after the study give another reduced conceptual framework excluding the variables and the relationships which were not supported by the results.

v) Diagrams or graphical illustrations aid better and quick understanding of relationships between variables.

Relationships in a conceptual framework

In the definition of a conceptual framework and even in the rationale of using a conceptual framework, the term relationship is dominantly featuring. To this end, there is need to examine what that term refers to in a conceptual framework. Relationship as used in a conceptual framework refers to the link that is postulated to subsist between the variables in a study. The relationship is usually illustrated by the use of arrows which can take two different forms. First, is the single directional arrow where the arrow moves from the influencers to the influenced variable. Second, is both directional arrow and double headed arrow where both variables are influencers to each other and at the same time influenced by each other.

However, it is important to note that the nature or magnitude or extent or level of influence is not depicted in the diagrammatical illustration of the variables. This can be established upon testing of the hypotheses formulated in a study, by either the findings of a study failing to reject the null hypothesis or the study findings rejecting the null hypothesis. The extent or magnitude or level of influence can be established by use of appropriate data analysis tools. Further, we also need to note that not all studies require establishment of the extent or magnitude or level of relationship between the variables under a study. However, this will be determined by the type of the research design the researcher will adopt in a study.

Also the independent variable constructs inter-relationship between them may be shown by use of arrows in a conceptual framework but in certain studies they may not be indicated by use of arrows although a researcher may go on and assess or establish their nature of relationship, extent of influence between them and the cumulative resultant nature of relationship or extent of influence on the dependent variable.

Researcher and conceptual framework

The development of a conceptual framework cannot be examined without analysis of the investigator in respect to his or her understanding of a phenomenon being investigated. Besides, in order to meet the purpose of research, the researcher should investigate the phenomenon in order to understand and explain it. In view of the foregoing, it is vital for the investigator to have some insights or at least some tentative understanding about the phenomenon under investigation.

The insights may be based on the investigator's own experience or understanding or on other experiences in conducting research. It is therefore important to note that the entry behaviour of the investigator is key in developing a conceptual framework. The knowledge of the phenomenon under investigation by the researcher can be informed through the researcher's ability to examine the existing theories, empirical studies, general literature review as well as business practices and principles among others.

To the researcher, whatever the source of insights, it would be vital in guiding the design, data collection for the study and determining the relevance or meaningfulness of the findings. Without such insights and tentative understanding by the researcher, the investigation may be a futile effort and meaningless.

A good researcher will be able to present the variables involved and the aspects in the phenomenon that is being investigated. This means that he should not only have an idea as to what factors may be involved but also an idea as to their nature and possible relationships.

A researcher is like a hunter in a hunting expedition to catch some kind of game, for him to succeed in catching the kind of game he requires, the hunter should have prior understanding regarding the kind of game to be caught, the kind of vegetation, the time the game moves for search of water and even what the hunting tools are including traps to be layed are useful in ensuring that the hunter is effective in the hunt. Such understanding enables the hunter to determine the most appropriate strategy in hunting and also enables him to tell after the expedition whether he has caught the kind of game he wanted. The same applies to a researcher, meaning some prior understanding of the phenomenon under study is vital not only for the researcher for the same reasons but also to enable the readers to appropriate and understanding the study.

The Premises of a conceptual framework

In the definition of a conceptual framework we noted that its design derives validity from the literature review. However, the literature review can be operationalized to generate the specifics of the base upon which a conceptual framework is founded. These include the following:

> i)   Existing theories
> ii)   Empirical studies
> iii)   General literature review
> iv)   Existing policies
> v)   Laws, rules and regulations
> vi)   Business practices or principles.

i) Existing theories

A researcher may examine the existing theories by evaluating the tenets, assumptions and delimitations of the applicability of the theories. Therefore, the researcher will be at a position to recast the variables he is interested in addressing, through the evaluation of results. The validity of the existing theories can as well be examined in the evaluation by the researcher.

ii) Empirical studies

The empirical studies remain an integral part in conceptualization of variables in a study. The past studies in the relevant subjects of interest to the researcher may be assessed to establish the existing gaps that can be presented in a diagrammatical form. The parameters of assessing the empirical studies involve scope of the studies, study design and data collections.

iii) Existing policies

In both the public and private sectors, a number of policies are existing in guiding the operations of the concerns.

These policies are human resource management policies, investment and dividend policies, disaster management policies, environment and development policies. Examination of these policies can be conducted by a researcher on the basis of the objectives of those policies, the "pillars" and the environment in which they are actionable. This will give insights to the researcher on practicality of the pre-set objectives and the dynamic nature of the environment in which they operate.

iv) General literature review

The general literature review refers to the process that a researcher undertakes to go through existing selected primary, secondary and tertiary sources of literature on an issue of interest. This concerted effort by the researcher is an attempt to examine how the issue he is interested in addressing has been documented by others and which aspects have not been comprehensively addressed. The researcher will identify such aspects to constitute the gaps his study may fill.

v) Laws, rules and regulations

The conduct of the people, organizations and governments call for the establishment of specific laws, rules and regulations as may be necessitated by their subjects. The need of the subjects, methods of implementation and the implementers as well as the ever changing environment in which they apply may call for evaluation. A researcher will then use the resultant aspects to identify the loose links that can be illustrated graphically.

vi) Business practices and principles

The competitive business environment which is constituted by regulators, financers, the government, individual players and organization units tend to have particular practices and principles. The tenet of the practices and principles can be examined, thus weaknesses and strengths can be identified, appropriate measures taken on the weaknesses and the strengths solidified through research.

Chapter Five

CONCEPTUAL FRAMEWORK
VARIABLES

Abstract

A variable is a measurable characteristic that assumes different values among the subjects. Operationally a variable is a measurement, for example performance as a variable can be stated as profit margins, efficiency levels, market share or loan portfolio. A variable can as well be conceptualized in the researcher's perspective. Variables are divided into two; key variables and control variables. When expressing constructs of any variable, a researcher should consider among other things, measurability of the construct, scope of the study and the research design.

Key Words

Conceptual framework and Variables.

Introduction

This chapter details the general definition of variable, operational and conceptualized definitions of a variable. It also gives classification of variables, factors a researcher should consider when generating constructs of a variable and examples of construct of variables.

Definition of a variable

A variable is a measurable characteristic that assumes different values among the subjects. It is the type of quality or attribute or character that may take-on more than one value. It is therefore a logical way of expressing a particular attribute in a subject. Some variables are attributes that are expressed quantitatively and categorically. For example, categorical customer satisfaction is expressed in repeat purchase, good mouthing or customer loyalty. Motivation expressed in respect to working conditions, employee promotion, or employee remuneration. Variables that are expressed quantitatively are age which is expressed in years or height is expressed in meters and weight in kilogrammes.

A variable also refers to the factors or forces that are measurable or constitutes a value in particular subjects. In any study, variables should be precisely identified and the respective measures appropriately stated.

Operational definition of variables

Operational definition of variables is the measurement of a variable. It is the description of the operation that will be used in measuring the variable and that operational definition of a variable may be stated quantitatively or categorically. For example, the operational definition of the variable "type of instruction" may be stated categorically as lecture, group discussion, individual tutoring or independent study. Also the variable "age" can be stated as number of years, or days.

Certain variables can also be operationalized by the use of indicators. Indicators are the observable evidence of the degree of presence or absence of the variable a researcher is interested in, for example, business performance can be indicated by profit or loss margins, the market share, or the market price per share. Financing also can be operationalized in reference to the source of funds and the cost of funds.

Conceptual definition of variables

Conceptual definition of a variable is a way of specifying precisely what a researcher means when we use a particular term to refer to available. In conceptualizing the definition of a variable, researchers rely on the premises on which the subject being conceptualized is based on. For example, distance is conceptualized as the number of kilometers covered, age is conceptualized as the period between the day one was born and the present date, that may be in years or months or days.

However, even with the existing bases, different researchers may still project different views on the conceptualization of the variables. For example, the variable internal control system can only be meaningful defined by reference to measurable concepts such as risk assessment, monitoring and evaluation, control activities and reporting systems. Such terms or variables happen to be a combination of several other concepts. The aspects which are used to conceptualize the variable internal control system are known as constructs or surrogates. The inclusion of such constructs in a study depends on the research design, scope of the study as well as the position that the surrogate occupies in a variable being conceptualized.

Classification of variables

Variables can be classified into two main categories namely:

    i) **Key variables** (Study Title Variables)
        a) Independent variable
        b) Dependent variable

    ii) **Control variables**
        a) Intervening variable

    b) Moderating or confounding or contextual variable.

    c) Antecedent variable

i) Key Variables (study title variables)

The key variables are those measurable characteristics that a researcher is interested in studying and they are presented in the title of any study. These variables are the independent and dependent variables.

a) *Independent variable*

The independent variable is also known as the influencer. It is a variable that calls for manipulation in a study for a behavior or change to be triggered in a dependent variable. The direction in which the independent variable is manipulated is likely to influence the dependent variable. The form or nature of influence generated through the manipulation of the independent variable can be measured by the aid of appropriate indicators of the dependent variable. In the design of a simple conceptual framework with only the key variables, the independent variable usually is on the left hand side while the dependent variable on the right hand side. The independent variable is key in any study and it should be carefully identified by the researcher through the review of literature or the six premises discussed in the previous chapters. For example, in a hypothetical study titled "effect of motivation on employee productivity in sugar firms in Kenya", the independent variable is motivation.

b) *Dependent variable*

The dependent variable is the influenced variable. This variable is the one that once the independent variable is manipulated, a change can be detected or no change can be indicated in the dependent variable. The indicators or measures of the dependent variable are unique in each area of study. For example, organization performance may have indicators such as market share, share price index in the stock market, profit margins, amount of losses incurred and efficiency levels. Employee productivity can be measured in terms of number of units produced or sold or customers served at a given time, or time taken to produce a unit of output or to serve a single customer, number of mistakes made in a particular proportion of work.

The dependent variable should be captured in the title of any study. It is on the right hand side in a simple conceptual framework illustrating the independent and dependent variables.

Fig. 5.1 Independent and Dependent Variables

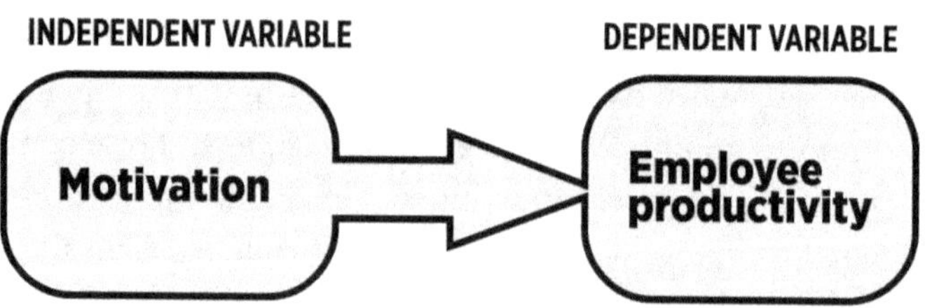

ii) **Control variables**

There are also other variables that may be presented in a conceptual framework in accordance to the researcher's scope of study. A researcher through literature review of theories and previous studies can identify the variables in a study. These variables can influence the results of a study where they are not controlled and they are also known as extraneous variables or concomitant, covariate or blocking variables. These variables include:

a) Intervening variable

The intervening variable is a link variable between the independent and dependent variables. In marketing and specifically placement, the intervening variable resembles the market intermediaries or middle - men who link the producers to the consumers in the market. The intervening variable explains or determines the kind of influence that the independent variable may have on the dependent variable. The manipulation of the independent variable can either be stepped up or down by the intervening variable and the resultant outcome influences the dependent variable.

The intervening variable should be appropriately identified by a researcher through in-depth literature review. For example, in a hypothetical study titled "Influence of internal control system on the financial management of SACCO in Kenya" may have an intervening variable as the control environment which is also referred to as the "tone at the top" In this example, the independent variable will be the internal control system, while dependent variable is financial management.

Fig. 5.2 Independent, Intervening and Dependent Variables

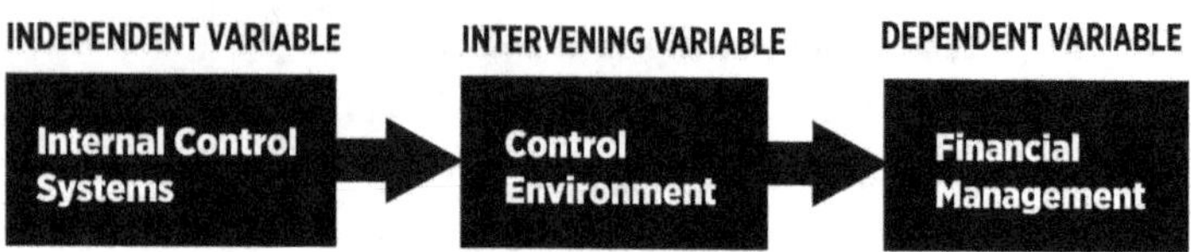

b) Moderating variable

Moderating variables can also be referred to as confounding or contextual variables. These variables are also having pseudo influence on the independent, intervening and dependent variables. Moderating variables may have a direct pseudo- influence on the dependent variable also. However, in the case of independent and intervening variables, the moderating variables have indirect influences on them. The resultant influence may impact on or affect the dependent variable. They moderate the relationship between the independent and dependent variable.

The moderating variables may water down the findings of a study and should be carefully identified and even their number should be checked. The identified ones should be very pertinent to the independent, intervening and dependent variables. In some studies, the confounding variables may be study setup based; as such they may be referred to as organizational factors such as organization structure, management style, employee skills and knowledge, financial framework of the organization as well as level of technology of the organization.

Fig. 5.3 Independent, Intervening, Moderating and Dependent variables

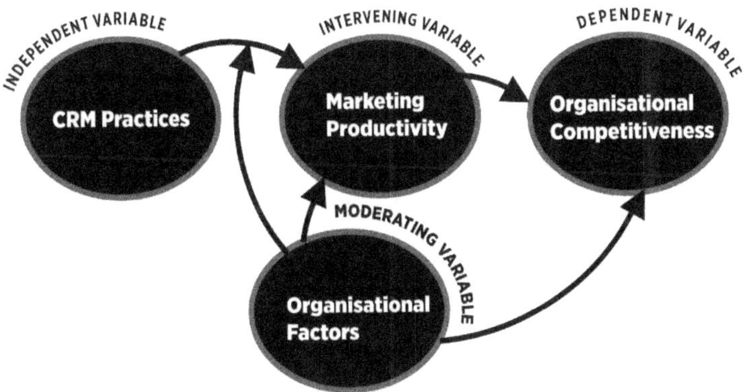

Source: Source: Thuo, K'ohonyo and Wainaina (2011)
Key CRM – Customer Relationship Marketing

c) Antecedent variable

While the intervening variable intervenes in the relationship between independent and dependent variables, antecedent variables catalise the influence that precedes such a relationship. Antecedent variable causes influence on the independent variable and because of the resultant influence, the independent variable will influence the dependent variable.

There are certain conditions to be met in classifying a variable as an antecedent variable. These are;

i) The variables, including antecedent variable must be related in some logical sequence.

ii) When the antecedent variables is controlled the relationship between the independent and the dependent variables should not disappear rather it should be enhanced, or reduced.

iii) When the independent variable is controlled or its influence removed, there should not be any relationship between the antecedent variable and dependent variable. Course-effect relationship may be used to explain the antecedent variable. In conceptualizing variables in a study, a researcher can start by examining theories in establishing cause effect description of a phenomenon which can consequently lead to other effects. It is like the multiplier effect of inflation on the economy or the famous vicious cycle of poverty; "If there is low savings, investment will be low and with low investments, production will reduce and with reduction in production, income will be low and this will lead to low savings. In this case, low savings antecedate on the investments and the resultant influence affect production and the sequence can continue over and over again.

Figure 5.4 Antecedent, Independent and Dependent Variables

Constructs of a variable

Constructs of a variable refers to the operationalized aspects of that variable or they are the tenets of a variable under study. The constructs are derived from the analysis or evaluation or application of a theory, business practices and principles or policies among others. To identify appropriate constructs of a variable a researcher should undertake comprehensive literature review in the relevant areas of study.

The term constructs are mainly associated with the independent, intervening, moderating and antecedent variables while in the case of the dependent variable we often use the term indicators of the dependent variable or the measures of the dependent variable.

Factors a researcher should consider when identifying or generating or assigning constructs to a variable

Researchers do not just assign constructs to a variable any-how from nowhere, but the constructs must come from somewhere. To this end, the scope of the study should be the first guiding principal when identifying or establishing constructs of a variable. The scope of a study provides the framework within which the study being conducted is revolving around. It limits the study to certain specifics in a study subject.

Second is the research design. The class of research is vital to be taken into account when assigning constructs to a variable. The researcher asks himself whether or not the study design will accommodate the constructs? For example, are the constructs relevant in cause-effect relationship or the causal comparative research design.

Third is the review of literature. The review of literature may involve both general and critical review of literature. This important exercise in research enlightens the researcher on the general tenets of a variable and the researcher will analytically assess these tenets in respect to the applicability in different set ups or time dynamics or policies and principles, technological advancements, disaster continuum model or business cycles. A researcher will be able to present variable constructs that measure upto the study issues or gaps.

Fourth is the theories. A constellation of theories are playing a key role in the identification of a research problem. Therefore, the review of the existing theories provides a researcher with an array of particular issues on the theory in different environments as well as salient features of the theory. A researcher will be able to come up with appropriate constructs upon assessing the above mentioned issues. For example, the classical economist (classical theory) believed that the economy is inherently stable and economic downturns can be easily corrected by the invisible hand of the market place. However, the great depression of the 1930s disapproved the invisible hand of the market place when it was unable to reverse the effects of the great depression. John Keynes wrote in 1935: "Classical economists were apparently unmoved by the lack of correspondence between the results of the theory and the facts of observation; a discrepancy which an ordinary man has not failed to observe..." Constructs that may be identified from this theory are: economic levers such as monetary and fiscal policies.

The measurement of the constructs is the fifth factor. These constructs should be capable of being measured by the indicators of the dependent variable. If they cannot be measured it may be hard to examine the influence they can bring on the dependent variable either directly or indirectly.

Examples of constructs of a variable

The examples will be presented in accordance to each type of variable that is the independent variable, moderating variable, intervening variable and antecedent variable. Besides, hypothetical study titles will be included in the presentation.

The Effect of Customer Service on the Organizational Performance of the Commercial Banks in Kenya

Independent variable: Customer service

Constructs of independent variable: - *Staff professionalism*
- *Nature of service delivery*
- *Customer feedback*
- *Premise layout*

Independent Variable: Organizational performance

Indicators of the Dependent variable:
- *Market share*
- *Corporate image*
- *Firms asset base*
- *Profit margins*

Intervening variable: Customer satisfaction

Constructs of intervening variable:
- *Repeat purchase*
- *Customer loyalty*
- *Willingness to pay premium price*
- *Mouthing*

Moderating variable:
Constructs of
moderating variables:

Organization factors

- Organization ownership
- *Size of the organization*
- *Level of technology*
- *Management style*

Influence of University Examinations on the Behavior of Students during Examination Weeks in the Kenyan Public Universities

Independent variable:
Constructs of
independent variable

University examinations
- *Type of examination*
(Qualitative or quantitative)
  - *Course work coverage*
- *Nature of Supervision in the examination room*
- *Teaching methodology*

Dependent variable:
Indicators of dependent
variable:

Behaviour of Students
- *Type of clothes worn*
  - *Scramble for specific sitting point in the exam room*
  - *Students attendance statistics in the library.*
  - *Students movement in the compound*
  - *Level of socialization*
  - *Facial appearance*
  - *Site preferred in preparing for*

exams

Moderating variable: Student factors

Constructs of
moderating variable:
- *Student entry behavior*
- *Extent of preparation for the examinations*
- *Peer influence*
- *Student culture.*

What is the Nature of Relationship Between Selected Determinant Factors and Dividend Policies of the Quoted Companies in Kenya?

Independent variable: Selected determinant factors.

Constructs of
independent variable: Financial position and performance:
- *Liquidity*
- *Profitability*

Shareholders expectations:
- *Clientele effect*
- *Loyalty*
- *Informational content*

Company financial needs:
- *Long term investments*
- *Short term investments*

Dependent variable: Dividend policies

Measures of
dependent variable:
- *Nature of dividend policy;*
- *Stable dividend policy*
- *Fluctuating dividend policy*

Moderating variables: *- Fiscal policy (taxation)*
- Government control
- Marketing policy

Measures or indicator of a dependent variable

A dependent variable is the character or attribute which is influenced by the independent variable or confounding variables existence or non-existence.   It is therefore necessary for a researcher to measure the nature of influence in the dependent variable through the manipulation of the independent variable. A researcher has to identified appropriate indications or measures as may be determined by the constructs of other variables more especially the constructs of the independent variable. For example, performance of the employee can be measured in terms of number of units produced, or customers served or level of efficiency.

Factors to consider when choosing measures of a dependent variable

The main thing to take into account when identifying indicators of a dependent variable is the constructs of the independent variable. First, it is vital to note that these constructs should be measured by use of appropriate indicators. In some cases a construct may take more than one indicators or just one indicator. In a study where a particular construct can only be measured by a single indicator, a researcher should directly link that constructs to the indicator when formulating the specific objectives of the study. For example, assume that a researcher would like to research on "effect of capital structure on the performance of listed sugar firms in the Nairobi stock exchange, Kenya". In this study, the independent variable is capital structure and the dependent variable is performance of listed sugar firms. The constructs of the independent variable are owners' capital, borrowed capital and the working capital. The indicators of performance of listed sugar firms can be market price per share, rate of dividend growth, market share, net income margins and level of efficiency. Now assume that owners' capital can only be measured by the rate of dividend growth, and then when the researcher will be designing the specific objectives, he can examine the influence of owners' capital on the rate of dividend growth of the listed sugar firms in the Nairobi stock exchange.

Second, the study setup may also determine the kind of indicators a dependent variable can have. For example, if a researcher would like to conduct a study on "influence of motivation on employee performance in the manufacturing firms in Kenya"; A case of cement manufacturing firms or if a researcher decides to investigate "influence of motivation on employee performance in the service firms in Kenya"; A case of commercial banks. In the two hypothetical studies, the independent variable is motivation while the dependent variable is employee performance. The constructs of the independent variable can be the working conditions, remuneration, recognition and promotion while these constructs can apply in both manufacturing and service firms, the indicators of employee performs in these two sectors may differ. For example, in the manufacturing firms, employee performance can be measured in terms of number of units produced or number of bags spoilt in ten units at a given time. However, in the service firms, the same can be measured in terms of number of customers served at a given time or number of customers poorly/ ineffectively served out of ten customers served, at a given time.

The indicators of dependent variables are usually predetermined and some can take standard forms such as profit or loss margins, level of efficiency and effectiveness, amount of work done at a given time, share price index, market share, earnings per share and size of the firm that is number of employees or number of branches or assets owned.

Chapter Six

FORMS OF CONCEPTUAL FRAMEWORK

Abstract

The two different forms of conceptual framework are a simple and a complex conceptual framework. The study title and the scope of a study occupy a special place in any form of conceptual framework. However, in determining whether a conceptual framework is simple or complex, the basis may be the relationships to be examined or established, study type, direction of the arrows, scope of the study, hypotheses to be tested in a study and the number of variables involved.

Key Word

Conceptual framework.

Introduction

This chapter describes the place of a study title and scope of the study in a conceptual framework. Types of conceptual framework, and their examples as well as the factors determining the simplicity and complexity of a conceptual framework are also discussed.

The place of a study title in a conceptual framework

In the design of a conceptual framework, a study title occupies a special place, because a good study title should precisely have the independent and dependent variables. These two variables are the foundation on which other variable derives their validity from.

A conceptual framework is defined as the diagrammatical presentation of the variables in a study as conceptualized by a researcher with the aid of analysis of the existing theories, business practices and principles, empirical studies, existing policies as well as the laws, rules and regulations. However, in some cases, it is not possible to have all the variables in a study carried in the title of a study but it is necessary that the independent and dependent variable to be explicitly expressed in any study title.

Place of the scope of a study in a conceptual framework

Among the qualities of a good statement of the research problem is the simplicity and preciseness of how the research problem is described. A good research problem should be specific and focused, clearly indicating the variables a researcher is interested in investigating and how they can be measured. To enhance the specificness of the research problem, in the scope of the study, the independent variable constructs should be precisely described and the dependent variable indicators appropriately identified.

Therefore, a conceptual framework seeks to presents the variables as identified in the study as well as their constructs and indicators, in a diagrammatical illustration. There could be a number of constructs in a particular independent variable but a researcher may only be interested in systematically investigating two or three constructs. The number of constructs may be determined by the position they occupy in a variable thus those constructs which occupy key positions in the independent variable under a study may be identified for investigation unlike those constructs which may be at the periphery of the variables under study.

They will then be neatly captured in a conceptual framework by a researcher as components of the diagram that will guide a study, and this is non other than a conceptual framework.

Types of conceptual framework

Conceptual frameworks are divided into two main forms namely;

      i)   *A simple conceptual framework*
    (ii) *A complex conceptual framework*

(i) A simple conceptual framework

Simple conceptual framework is the presentation of not more than three variables in a conceptual framework, and also the arrows linking constructs of the independent variable if any are single directional. For example, a simple conceptual framework may contain independent, moderating and dependent variables or independent, intervening and dependent variables or simply the independent and dependent variables only.

Example of simple conceptual frameworks
In giving the examples of a simple conceptual framework a number of hypothetical study titles will be used as a guide as follows:

Factors influencing girl child education in primary schools among the pastoralist communities in Kenya

Fig. 6.1: The Conceptual Framework of Pastoralist Communities Influencing Factors and Girl Child Education

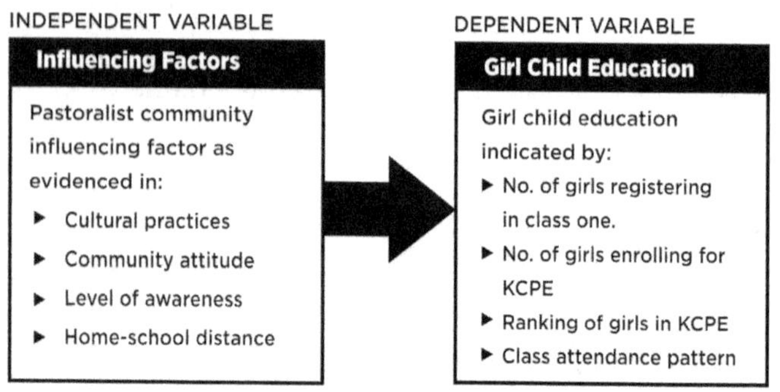

Source: Self Conceptualization (2019)

The researcher has conceptualized his study on two variables, that is, pastoralists community factors and girl child education. The pastoralists community factors are evidenced through; cultural practices, community attitude, level of awareness and, home- school distance. The girl child education is indicated by the number of girls registering in class one, number of girls enrolling for KCPE, ranking of girls in KCPE and class attendance pattern.

Determinant of African economic problems; a case of east African countries

In this fact finding study, the researcher wishes to investigate the causes of African economic problems. These causes are;

Fig.6.2 The Conceptual Framework of Determinant Factors.

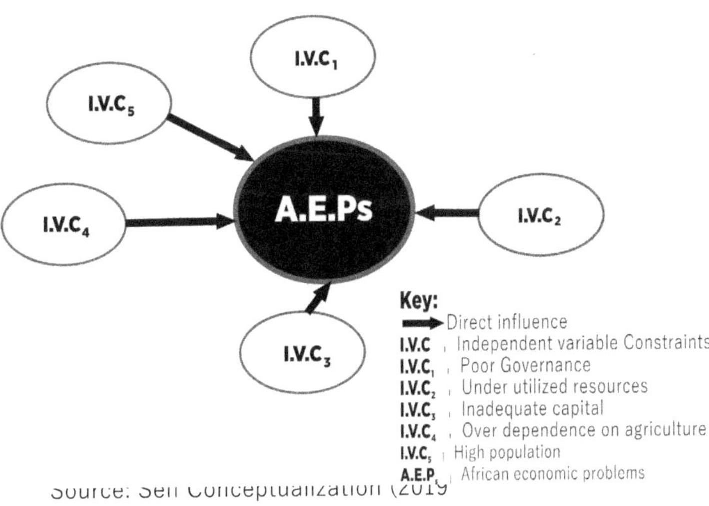

Source: Self Conceptualization (2019)

poor governance, under utilized resources, inadequate capital, over dependence on agriculture and high population. African economic problems can be assessed through; mortality rates, dependency ratio, political instability, rate of crime, industrial absorption rate and teacher–pupil ratio.

The researcher is merely interested in identifying the determinants of the African economic problems and he does not go beyond that by examining for example, investigating the effect of the determinants on the economic growth of the selected countries.

Impact of HIV and AIDS on the household income of the Luo community in Kenya

Fig. 6.3: The Conceptual Framework of HIV and AIDS Causes and Household Income.

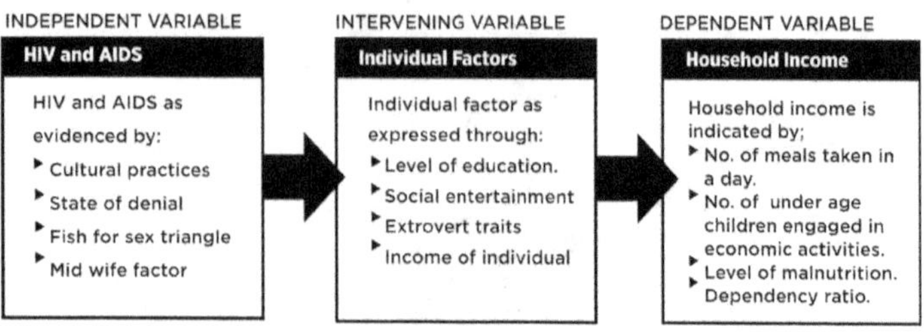

Source: Self Conceptualization (2019)

Conceptually, HIV and AIDS impact on household income has been expressed through examination of the causes of HIV and AIDS as evidenced by; cultural practices, state of denial, fish for sex triangle and mid–wife factors, while household income is indicated by; number of meals taken in a day, number of underage children engaged in economic activities, level of malnutrition and depending ratio. The relationship between HIV and AIDS causes and the household income is intervened by the individual factors which are expressed in terms of level of education, income of an individual, social entertainment and extrovert traits.

Customer service practices and customer satisfaction: An empirical study of the commercial banks in Kenya

Figure 6.4 Present the relationship between customer service practices and customer satisfaction in the commercial banks in *Fig 6.4.* The Conceptual Framework of Customers Service Practices and Customer Satisfaction.

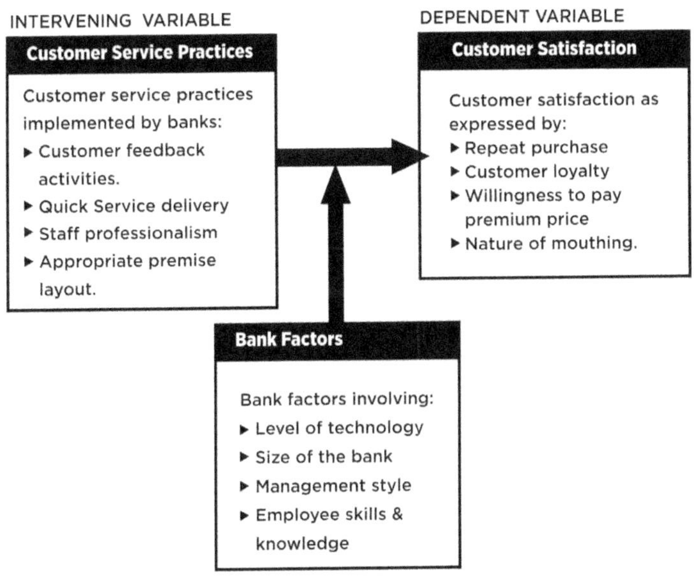

Source: Self-Conceptualization (2019)

Kenya. The relationship is moderated by a number of bank factors. Customer service practices are implemented through customer feedback activities, quick service delivery, staff professionalism and appropriate premise layout, while customer satisfaction is expressed by the repeat purchase, customer loyalty, customers' willingness to pay premium price as well as nature of mouthing. The bank factors are management style, size of the bank, level of technology and employee skills and knowledge. The manipulation of the customer service practices are presumed to influence customer satisfaction, however, bank factors can moderate the nature of relationship between customer service practices and customer satisfaction.

Capital Structure and Organizational Performance of listed Firms at the Nairobi Stock Market, Kenya.

Fig. 6.5 The Conceptual Framework of Capital Structure Composition and Organizational Performance.

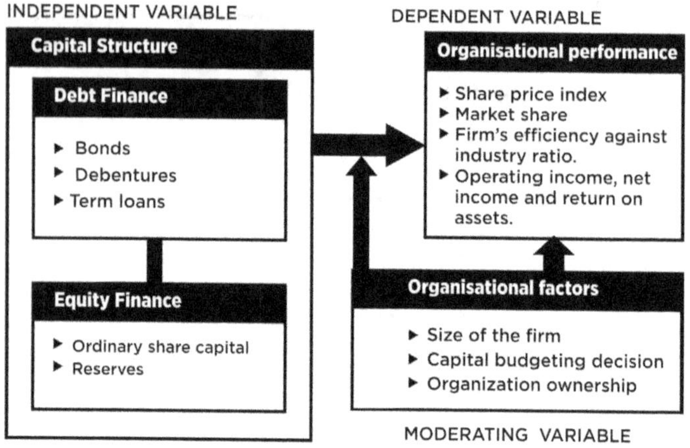

Source: Self Conceptualization (2019)

The researcher would like to investigate the relationship between the capital structure composition as exhibited by debt and equity finance, while organizational performance will be measured in terms of share price index, market share, firm's efficiency against industry ratio and operating income, net income and return on assets. The relationship is moderated by organizational factors; size of the firm, capital budgeting decision and organization ownership. Besides, the researcher will establish the effect of organization factors on the performance of organizations.

(ii)   A complex conceptual framework

A complex conceptual framework is that type of conceptual framework that contains more than three variables. Also such conceptual framework may have the constructs of the independent variable link by double headed arrows hypothesizing a relationship between the constructs linked which the researcher is required to examine. Besides, in some studies all the variables presented in a conceptual framework are linked to one another as illustrated in figure 6.6.

The complexity of a conceptual framework is determined by the scope of a study which is also guided by the gap that a researcher would like to fill in his study. For example, a researcher may be interested in establishing the nature of relationship subsisting between the variables, level of influence of constructs of a variable on another variable, as well as the cause and effect relationship.

What is the effect of internal control systems on performance of savings and credit cooperative societies in Kenya?

The conceptual framework in figure 6.6 present the effect of the activities of internal control system on the performance of SACCOs but this effect is intervened by the control environment and moderated by three SACCO factors; size of the SACCO, age of the SACCO and composition of the members. The activities of the internal control systems are categorized into accounting and administrative controls, control environment is expressed through organizational culture, structure, philosophy, management style and management overrides,

Fig. 6.6: The Conceptual Framework of the Internal Control System Activities and Performance of Saccos.

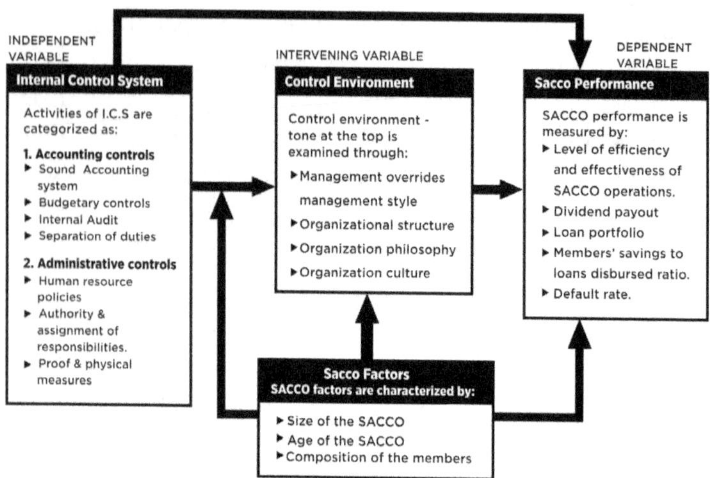

Source: Self Conceptualization (2019)

The performance of SACCOs are measured through level of efficiency and effectiveness of SACCO operations, dividend payout, loan portfolio, default rate, members' savings to loans disbursed ratio.

Factors determining the simplicity and complexity of a conceptual framework

A number of factors determine whether a conceptual framework is simple or complex, and these factors are as follows:

   i) Scope of the study
   ii) Relationships to be examined

iii)   Hypotheses to be tested in the study
iv)   Fact finding studies
v)   Direction of the arrow
vi)   Direct or/and indirect influence
vii)   Number of variables in a study
viii)   Other factors

i) The scope of the study

The scope of a study helps in providing the boundary within which a study is conducted. It does not only consider the organization or community or regional set-up of a study but more so the constructs of the independent variable. The nature of those constructs and how they are designed can determine the form of a conceptual framework.

The scope is crafted from the theory or documented issues which the researcher is interested in examining to identify the gaps that the study at hand can bridge. The general review of literature shows how the issue at hand has been studied or presented by others in the documented literature. It commences from the broader perspective to the critical review where gaps are shown by the researcher.

ii) Relationship to be examined or established

A researcher may be interested in examining the nature of relationship that exists between the variables in a study as well as the constructs of a particular variable more special the independent variable. These relationships will determine the aspects that a conceptual framework should illustrate hence determining its complexity or simplicity. For example, when a researcher is interested in investigating the relationship between the constructs of the independent variable he is likely to complicate the conceptual framework.

iii) Hypotheses to be tested in a study.

A hypothesis is defined as a tentative answers to a research problem which may postulate the existence or non existing of relationships. Hypotheses are of two types; null hypothesis and alternative hypothesis. Null hypothesis postulates that there is no relationship that exists between the variables of a study, while alternative hypothesis presupposes that indeed relationships subsist between the variables of a study. Alternative hypothesis can either be directional or non directional.

The number of hypotheses formulated for testing can determine the simplicity or complexity of a conceptual framework. Where there are many hypotheses to be tested the conceptual framework is likely to be complex, unlike when there are only a few or one hypothesis to be tested. A good conceptual framework should show the hypotheses to be tested in a study.

iv) Fact-finding studies

Fact finding studies are also known as primitive research and they are less advanced as compared to pure research. These studies are merely interested in finding out factors affecting the dependent variable. For example, if a researcher is investigating factors affecting food production in Eastern part of Kenya.

After the researcher has identified these factors affecting food production, the study ends there. He does not go further to examine how the identified factors affect food production and even analyze their level of influence which may be scaled.

A two variable conceptual framework more often presents fact finding studies and such studies are associated with the simple form of a conceptual framework.

v) Direction of the arrow

Double headed directional arrows in a conceptual framework can make the conceptual framework complex unlike in a case where arrows are single directional. In the double head directional arrows, the researcher aims at examining or establishing the influence from one variable to another as well as from one construct to another and vice versa.

vi) Direct or indirect influence

In a case where there is an intervening variable, the independent variable may not have a direct influence on the dependent variable but will present indirect influence through the intervening an variable. Also moderating variable influencing an intervening variable and the resultant influence then influences the dependent variable. These indirect influences are mostly associated with complex conceptual frameworks.

vii) The number of variables

The more the variables are in a conceptual framework the more complex the conceptual framework. A simple conceptual framework contains between two to three variables, while a complex conceptual framework contains between four to five variables. The number of variables coupled with the direction of arrows and the number of hypotheses formulated for testing make a conceptual framework complex.

ix) Other factors

A conceptual framework varies according to levels, depending on the phenomenon being studied, how the problem has been defined, the research objectives and the level of conceptualization by a researcher, that is, how a researcher has understood the phenomenon or in other words perceived the issue being investigated.

Chapter Seven

CONCEPTUAL FRAMEWORK AND RESEARCH OBJECTIVES

Abstract

A conceptual framework can guide the formulation of both the broad objective and specific objectives in a study. The objectives of any study should be SMART and they should be formulated using non-biased verbs such as investigate, examine, assess, determine or explore. The approaches that can be used when stating the purpose and objectives of a study are of two types; the first approach is where a researcher uses the constructs of the variable more especially the independent variable constructs, while the second approach involves the use of the variable itself like organizational factors or motivation.

Key Words

Conceptual framework and Objectives.

Introduction

The chapter details the definition of study objectives, verbs used when stating the purpose and objectives of a study, qualities of a good study objectives, formulating objectives with the aid of a conceptual framework, approaches of stating the purpose and objectives of a study as well as the study objectives, questionnaires and questionnaire items.

Definition of research objectives

A research objective is what a researcher intends to achieve at the end of the study by assessing specific aspects of a phenomenon under investigation. Research objectives are of two types namely:

      (i)   Broad objective

      (ii)   Specific objectives

i) Broad objective

This is a broad statement of what the study seeks to achieve. The statement of the research problem is the origin of the broad objective. A researcher should state precisely the broad objective of a study he is interested in investigating. The broad objective of a study presents both the independent and the dependent variables in a study title, as well as other variables may be carried in a study title.

ii) Specific objectives

A broad objective can be operationalized to generate the specific objectives by referring to the specific aspects of a phenomenon under study which a researcher desires to bring out at the end of the study. In short, the specific objectives are derived from the purpose of the study and the purpose of the study is generated from the statement of the research problem. Where a gap in a study is expressed in the form of research questions, the objectives of the study can also be formulated from the research questions. It should be well thought out in order to capture the aspects of central theme of the study, clearly and logically linking the specific objectives to the dependent variable or its indicators accordingly.

Verbs used in stating of purpose or objectives of a study.

A verb is a word or group of words that expresses action, an event or a state. In research, expression of aspects of a phenomenon by use of words that state the variable or its constructs is necessary.

The verbs used in stating the purpose of a study should be neutral or non biased. Examples of such verbs are;

a) To investigate
b) To establish
c) To examine
d) To explore
e) To compare
f) To differentiate
g) To assess
h) To analyze
i) To test
j) To inquire
k) To find out

The use of biased verbs should be discouraged by researchers in formulating statements of purpose and objectives of a study. Examples of such verbs are namely:

a) To show
b) To validate
c) To prove
d) To indicate
e) To confirm
f) To explain
g) To illustrate
h) To demonstrate
i) To check

Qualities of a good research objective;

A good research objective should posses the following characteristics.

i) Objective should be clearly well written and precise.

ii) Objective should be specific, significant, realistic and achievable.

iii) Objective should flow logically from statement need and address the problem.

iv) Objective should fall within the range of results, which are expected to be achieved within the limit of time, money and human resource available.

v) Objective should be stated as far as possible allowing measurement or at least observation of their achievement.

vi) Should be stated hierarchically and/or chronologically.

In summary the objectives should be SMART, that is specific, measurable, achievable, realistic and time bound. The specification is in reference to the connection to the scope of the study. Every objective should allow for development of indicators or measurements, or they should be capable of being evaluated. The possibility of achieving a particular objective depends partly on the resources available and the duration of the project. Avoid being too ambitious by stating objectives that sound unrealistic in view of the state of knowledge on the subject and resources available. Time element is crucial and the study should be completed within a specified period.

Formulating objectives with the aid of a conceptual framework

The appropriate aspects of a phenomenon under a study can be presented in a conceptual framework which a researcher will use in formulating the study objectives. For example, the independent variable and the dependent variable will assist in formulating the broad objective or the purpose of the study. Also the aspects of the independent variable can be used in formulating the specific objectives.

Assume that a researcher is interested in investigating the influence of motivation on employee performance in the cement manufacturing firms in Kenya. In this hypothetical study title, a conceptual framework can be used to guide the formulation of the research objectives. The aspects of motivation can be working conditions, employee remuneration and promotion of employee. The indicators of employee productivity can be number of units produced at a given time, number of units spoilt in a given quantity of output, level of innovativeness of an employee. The moderating variable could be organizational factors which can be measured by: management style, skills and knowledge of an employee, technological level of the firm and organizational structure.

The above described aspects of the phenomenon can be diagrammatically summarized and presented in the conceptual framework in figure 7.1 below.

Effect of Motivation on Employee Performance in the Cement Manufacturing Firms in Kenya.

The conceptual framework in figure 7.1, presents a condensed description of the phenomenon to be studied by examining

Fig 7.1: The Conceptual Framework of Motivation and Employee Performance

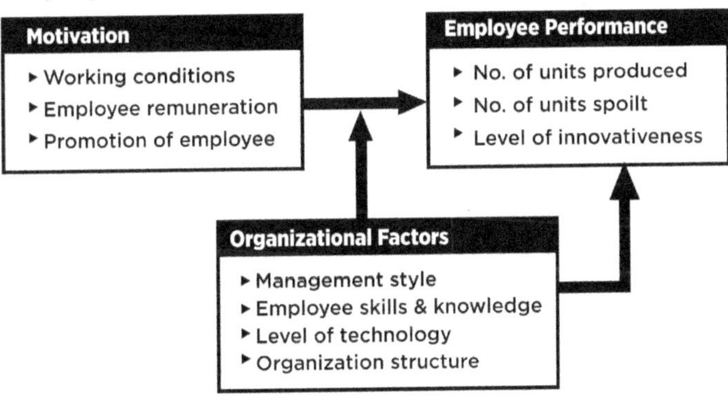

Source: Self Conceptualization (2019)

the influence of motivation on the employee performance in the cement manufacturing firms in Kenya. The researcher would like to assess the effect of identified motivational factors; working conditions, employee remuneration and promotion on the performance of an employee. Employee performance will be measured in terms of the number of units produced or number of units spoilt in a given quantity of out put as well as the level of innovativeness of an employee. The researcher will further examine the influence of organizational factors on the relationship between motivation and employee performance. Again the researcher would like to investigate the direct influence of organizational factors on the performance of an employee.

Approaches of stating the purpose and objectives of a study

There are three approaches a researcher can use when stating the purpose and objectives of the study namely:

A. First approach; specific constructs

Purpose of the study

The purpose of this study is to investigate the contribution of motivation on employee performance in the cement manufacturing firms in Kenya.

Objectives of the study

Specifically the study seeks:

i) To examine the effect of working conditions on employee performance.

ii) To assess the contribution of remuneration on employer performance

iii) To determine the influence of employee promotion on employee performance.

iv) To establish the effect of organizational factors on employee performance.

v) To establish the nature of relationship between motivation and employee performance.

vi) To determine the effect of organizational factors on the relationship between motivation and employee performance.

It is vital to note that different approaches can be adopted when formulating research objectives with the aid of a conceptual framework.

B. Second approach: compounded variables

The second approach is where a researcher links each of the variables to the dependent variable or moderating variable to the independent variable then to the dependent variable. This approach can generate the following objectives.

The broad objective of the study

The broad objective of this study is to investigate the effect of motivation on employee performance in the cement manufacturing firms in Kenya.

Specifically the study seeks:

i)   To examine the effect of motivational factors on employee performance.

ii) To assess the influence of organizational factors on employee performance.

iii) To determine the effect of organizational factors on the relationship between motivation and employee performance.

iv) To establish the nature of relationship between motivation and employee performance.

v)   To determine the nature of relationship between organizational factors and the employee performance.

C. Third approach; specific measurements.

Again it is important to draw your attention to another approach of formulating objectives with the assistance of a conceptual framework. The third approach is where the aspects of the independent variable can be strictly measured by a particular indicator of the dependent variable. For example, if working conditions can only be measured by number of units produced at a given time then the researcher can directly link working conditions and number of units produced. Also if we can assume that the manipulation of employee remuneration can be measured in terms of level of innovativeness and employee promotion measured by the number of units spoilt in a given quantity of out put, then we can match the two constructs to their respective indicators in the dependent variable.

Purpose of the study

The purpose of this study is to investigate the impact of motivation on employee performance in the cement manufacturing firms in Kenya.

Objective of the study

Specifically the study seeks:

i) To examine the effect of working conditions on the number of units produced by an employee

ii) To assess the influence of employee remuneration on the level of innovativeness of an employee.

iii) To determine the contribution of employee promotion on the number of units spoilt in a given quantity by an employee.

iv) To establish the influence of organizational factors on the relationship between motivation and employee performance.

v) To examine the effect of organizational factors on employee performance.

Research objectives and constructing of questionnaires as well as questionnaire items

Questionnaires are among the most common research instruments in social science survey technique besides interview schedules, observational forms, standardized tests and records survey. Questionnaire is a set of carefully selected and ordered questions needed in survey studies to obtain important information about the population. Each item in the questionnaire is developed to address a specific objective, research question or hypothesis of a study.

Objectives should be listed first before constructing a questionnaire, where each item must relate to a certain objective. For example, in the first approach of formulating research objectives, the specific objective (i) which was examining the effect of working conditions on employee performance, the items that could be identified under this specific objective are; availability of the working tools state of the working tools, employee-working tool ratio, working space, nature of supervision, working relation among the employees and aeration of the working room or area.

The identified items from the stated objective will assist a researcher to construct a questionnaire that will contain different kind of questions such as structured or closed ended and unstructured or open ended or contingency questions or matrix questions.

Chapter Eight

CONCEPTUAL FRAMEWORK AND RESEARCH HYPOTHESES

Abstract

A study hypothesis in a prediction of some sort regarding the possible outcome of a study. Levels of hypothesis are three; the lowest level, relatively higher level and highest level. Sources of hypothesis are many; personal and idiosyncratic experience of a researcher, findings from other studies or a body of theory. Hypothesis is a declarative statement suggesting no effect, no change, things remain the same or there is no relationship between them. Also the statement can suggest there is an effect or change or there is a relationship between the variables. Hypothesis should be formulated in such a manner that the deductions can be made from it and that consequently a decision can be reached as to whether the hypothesis does or not explain the facts considered. The main purpose of hypothesis is to bridge the gap between the problem and the evidence needed through provision of direction by hypothesis. Hypotheses are of two types; alternative and null hypotheses. Hypotheses to be tested can be shown in a conceptual framework by use of arrows which can be marked as Ho1, Ho2, or Ho1a.

Key Words

Conceptual framework and Research hypotheses.

Introduction

This chapter contains definition of a study hypothesis, level of hypothesis, sources of hypothesis, elements of a study hypothesis, characteristics, purpose and types of hypothesis. Also included in the chapter are the advantages and disadvantages of using hypothesis in a study as well as formulating and presenting hypothesis in a conceptual framework.

Definition of research hypothesis

Research hypothesis is a prediction of some sort regarding the possible outcome of a study. Hypothesis is a researcher's anticipated explanation or opinion regarding the result of a study. It is a tentative answer to a research problem presented in a declarative statement of a relationship between two or more variables assumed to hold true. The aim of hypothesis in research is to confirm or disapprove the statement.

Hypothesis is a proposition, condition or principle that is assumed, perhaps without belief to draw out its logical consequences and by this method to test that it is accorded with facts that are known or may be determined.

Levels of hypothesis

Hypothesis can be classified into three levels; at the lowest level, we have hypothesis that state existence of certain empirical uniformities. An example is "East African men in the rural areas get married at the age of 22 to 24 years" At this level, hypothesis invites scientific verification of rather common sense propositions.

At a relatively higher level, we may have hypothesis centered on complex "ideal types". An example is a set of hypothesis regarding the characteristics of minorities in a society. At highest level, hypotheses are based on the relationship of analytical variables. Such hypotheses are normally statements about how changes in one variables do or do not explain observations in another variable. It is this higher level of hypothesis that a conceptual framework presents.

Sources of hypothesis

In establishing hypothesis there is need to obtain background information about the research problem area through literature review. A list of all possible causes or effects or solutions to the problem is prepared and those unlikely removed from the list. The remaining are refined to hypothesis statement that establish or lead to determining the data needed. To solve the problem one needs to be thorough, comprehensive and avoid overlooking any fact and then write the hypothesis in a declarative statement. Literature review by a researcher can be aided through the following:

i)   Personal and idiosyncratic experience of a researcher.

ii)   Analogies such as those comparing biological organisms with society, natural law with social law and thermodynamics with social dynamics.

iii)   Findings from other studies.

iv)   Hypothesis can be developed from a body of theory, you can construct hypothesis by logical deduction from theory.

The above listed sources of hypothesis are also the same premises on which conceptual framework variables are generated.

Elements of a research hypothesis

A research hypothesis has three main elements namely:

a)   Are declarative statements; suggesting no effect, no change, things remain the same or there is no relationship between them. Also the statement can suggest there is an effect or change or there is a relationship between the variables.

b) Are predictive statements; hypothesis tends to be forward looking (futuristic) providing guiding principles to the case of the whole research.

c) Containing clear elements of testing and verification that can be measured empirically or quantitatively.

Characteristics of a good hypothesis

i) Hypothesis should be formulated in such a manner that deductions can be made from them and that consequently a decision can be reached as to whether the hypothesis does or not explain the facts considered.

ii) Hypothesis must be conceptually clear. Concepts embodied in the hypothesis should be defined in a manner most commonly accepted and easily communicated.

iii) Hypothesis should be specific and must contain clear statements. For example, a variable like "social class" ought to be narrowed down to "education" or "income".

iv) Hypothesis should be related to a body of theory or some theoretical orientation. This requirement concerns the theoretic rationale of a hypothesis. If an hypothesis is related to some theoretical base, research will then help to qualify, support, correct or refute the theory.

v) Hypothesis should be related to available analytical techniques. A researcher who does not know what techniques are available to test an hypothesis is in a poor position to formulate usable questions. The above five characteristics of a good hypothesis can be summarized as precise and clear, within the context of their research area, conceptually clear, specific and clearly related to the general scope and purpose of the study, consistent with substantial body to establish facts and testable empirically.

Purpose of hypotheses

In a study, research hypotheses play a major role as explained below:

i)   They bridge the gap between the problem and the evidence needed for its situation through the provision of direction by hypotheses.

ii)   Hypotheses form the framework for the ultimate conclusions as solutions. Researchers usually base their conclusions on the results of the tests of their hypotheses.

iii)   Hypotheses sensitize the investigator to certain aspects of the situation that are relevant regarding the problem at hand.

iv)   Hypotheses enable the investigator to assess the information he has to collect from standpoint of both relevance and organization.

Type of hypotheses

A conceptual framework can present that one variable is related to another variable; this statement of relation is referred to as an alternative hypothesis. This can further be divided into two; directional hypothesis and non directional hypothesis which a researcher seeks to support. The alternative hypothesis which postulates that a relationship subsist between the variables under investigation. That relationship postulated can be expressed directionally or non-directionally.

An alternative directional hypothesis is where a researcher predicts the nature of the presumed subsisting relationship between the variables in a study.

An alternative directional hypothesis specifies the nature of the relationship or direction between variables. This means that a relationship may be stated as being positive, negative, strong, weak, greater than, less than, increased, decreased, higher than or lower than.

For example, an alternative directional hypothesis can be formulated as:

i) There is a positive relationship between the working conditions and employee performance.

ii) There is a high influence of working conditions on employee performance.

iii) There is significantly no relationship between working conditions and employee performance.

iv) There is a negative relationship between working conditions and employee performance.

In the alternative non directional hypothesis, the researcher remains neutral in formulating the hypothesis by simply recognizing that indeed a relationship subsists but whether that relationship is positive or negative, or whether it is strong or weak is not declared.

An alternative non-directional hypothesis is also known as a research hypothesis. This type of hypothesis states that there is a relationship or differences but the researcher does not know the nature of such differences or relationships. Stating a hypothesis in non- directional form is a conservative approach by a researcher in avoiding commitment to a specific outcome. A researcher states that a relationship exists between the variables but he does not indicate the direction of that relationship; whether it is high or low as stated in the example that follows.

For example, non-directional alternative hypothesis can be stated as:

i)   There is significant relationship between the working conditions and employee performance.

ii)   There is significant effect of the working conditions on employee performance.

The second type of hypothesis is a null hypothesis. It is a statistical proposition which states essentially that there is no relationship between the variables under study. Null hypothesis measures a status quo no significant change and it is the statistical hypothesis that a researcher seeks to reject.
For example, we can state the null hypothesis as;

i)   There is no relationship between the working conditions and employee performance.

ii)   There is no effect of the working conditions on employee performance.

Advantages of using a research hypothesis in a study

If a researcher uses research hypotheses in a study, the researcher is able to:

i) Think deeply about a possible outcome of the study,

because the predictions carried in the hypothesis postulates possible outcomes.

ii)   Make specific predictions based on the prior evidence or theoretical argument.

iii)   Assess whether a study is investigating a relationship between the study variables.

Disadvantages of using a research hypothesis in a study

Even though research hypothesis play a major role in a study, they may have certain demerits namely:

i)   The hypothesis may lead to bias on the part of a researcher or investigator either consciously or unconsciously.

ii)   A researcher may be tempted to arrange the procedure or manipulate the data so as to get the target outcome.

iii)   A researcher's attention may be concentrated on the prediction and may over look other phenomenon that may be vital to a study.

Formulation and presentation of research hypotheses in a conceptual framework.

In formulation of research hypotheses, a researcher may adopt different approaches just as what we presented in chapter seven of this book on the formulation of the research objectives. This demonstrates postulated link that may subsist between research objectives and hypotheses, in fact a good proposal, project or thesis should ensure that there is coherence between the research objectives and the hypotheses. Formulated hypotheses may be presented in the conceptual framework to illustrate the two approaches of formulating research hypotheses.

In order to enhance coherence between the research

objectives and hypotheses, the book is going to use a similar hypothetical study that was used in formulating research objectives with the guide of a conceptual framework of figure 7.1 in chapter seven of this book. Besides, the book will adopt both null and alternative hypotheses.

EXAMPLE I

Effect of Motivation on Employee Performance in the Cement Manufacturing Firms in Kenya

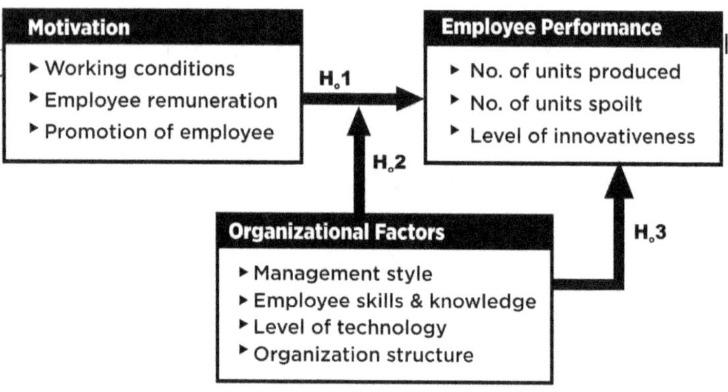

Source: Self Conceptualization (2019)

First Approach: Null Hypothesis

- **Ho1:** There is no effect of motivation on the employee performance or
- **Ho2:** There is no relationship between motivation and employee performance.

Under this aggregate hypothesis a number of other hypotheses can be formulated for testing, if the researcher is interested in predicting relationships between each of the motivational factors and employee performance. These include:

i) There is no influence of working conditions on employee performance.

ii) There is no relationship between employee remuneration and employee performance.

iii) There is no effect of promotion of employee on employee performance.

- **Ho2:** There is no effect of organizational factors on the relationship between motivation and employee performance.
- **Ho3:** There is no influence of organizational factors on employee performance.

EXAMPLE II

The conceptual framework and hypothesis is also illustrated by Thuo, J.K. Kibera, F.N. K'Ohonyo, P.O and Wainaina G. in a study titled "Customer Relationship Marketing and Competitiveness of Commercial Banks in Kenya" The study was based on the premises that customer relationship marketing practices influence organizational competitiveness but this influence is intervened by marketing productivity and moderated by a number of organizational factors namely, age, size and ownership of the organization; type of customer market being served, corporate reputation, duration of customer relationship marketing implementation and the technology level in the organization. The conceptual framework and hypotheses explaining the relationship among these variables is shown in figure 5.2.

Fig. 8.2: Conceptual Framework of CRM Practices and Organizational Competitiveness.

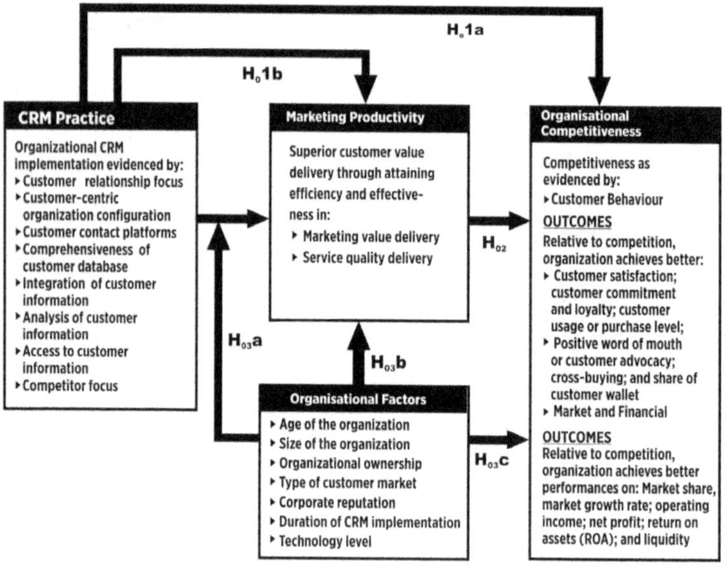

Source : Thuo et al (2011)

Note: **CRM** – Customer Relationship Marketing
The researchers formulated the following null hypothesis for testing from the conceptual framework in figure 5.2:

- **Ho1a:** There is no relationship between the banks' customer relationship marketing practices and their competitiveness.

- **Ho1b:** There is no relationship between the banks' customer relationship marketing practices and their marketing productivity.

- **Ho2:** There is no relationship between the banks' marketing productivity and their competitiveness.

- **Ho3a:** Organizational factors do not affect the relationship between the banks' customer relationship marketing practices and their marketing productivity.

- **Ho3b:** Organizational factors do not impact the banks' marketing productivity.

- **Ho3c:** Organizational factors do not influence the banks' competitiveness.

EXAMPLE III
Factors Affecting Quality of Free Primary Education in Kenya

The topic presents a fact-finding study like which is merely interested in establishing the cause-effect relationship between influencing factors and quality of free primary education in Kenya. The cause factors are; teacher-pupil ratio, inadequate learning facilities, gross understaffing, lack of commitment by some teachers and lack of mobile schools. The indicators of quality of free primary education are; mean score per subject, mean score in aggregate, proportion of pupils failing to the total number of registered candidates, congestion in class rooms, pupil- desk ratio and teacher- pupil feedback time.

Fig. 8.3: The Conceptual Framework of Causal Factors and Quality of Free Primary Education

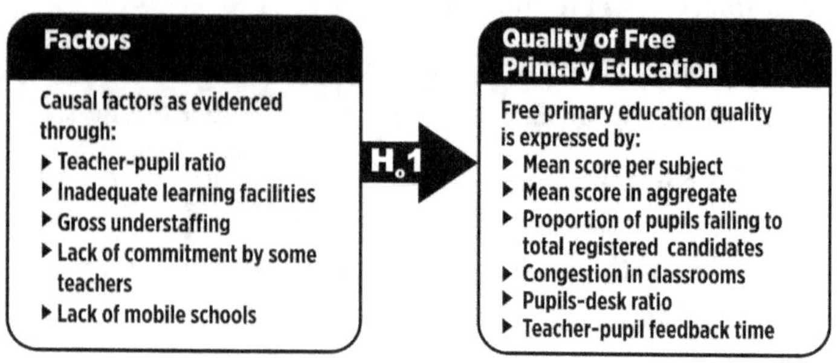

Source: Self conceptualization (2019)

In the conceptual framework in figure 5.3, the following null hypothesis can be formulated for testing:

- **Ho1:** There is no influence of causal factors on quality of free primary education in Kenya.

The researcher can as well formulate specific hypothesis for each of the identified causal factors for testing as follows;

i) Teacher-pupil ratio does not influence quality of free primary education.

ii) There is no relationship between inadequate learning facilities and quality of free primary education.

iii) There is no influence of gross understaffing on quality of free primary education.

iv) Lack of commitment by some teachers does not influence quality of free primary education.

v) There is no influence of lack of mobile schools on quality of free primary education.

Chapter Nine

THE CONCEPTUAL FRAMEWORK AND RESEARCH QUESTIONS

Abstract

Research questions in a study are the ones that the researcher would like to answer by conducting a study. Research questions provide direction by assisting in showing the identified gaps and such questions must be feasible, clear, significant and ethical. Research questions can be generated from the objectives of a study or and constructs of a study variable.

Key Words

Conceptual Framework and Research Questions.

Introduction

This chapter presents the meaning, purpose and qualities of a good research questions. It also outlines conceptualized variable constructs and the research questions as well as research questions - construction of questionnaires and questionnaire items.

Meaning of Research Questions

Research questions are the presented questions in the study that a researcher would like to be answered by conducting the study. In the statement of the research problem where the researcher identifies the gaps that his study would like to bridge can be presented by use of questions. The questions will constitute the research questions of the study.

Purpose of Research Questions

The following are the purpose of research questions in a study:

i) Research questions just like the hypothesis, they provide direction by assisting in the gap identification.

ii) In the background of the study where the study case is built by identifying the symptoms of the problem to be investigated and gathering of appropriate information to describe the phenomenon, questions posed in the statement of the research problem are best in summarizing these.

iii) The research questions help the researcher to understand the problem with greater clarity and use data collected to answer the questions.

iv) The research questions enlighten the researcher of the issues that are relevant regarding the problem under investigation.

v) The research questions are useful in the preparation of the research instrument for data collection.

vi) When the objectives formulated by the researcher are broader, then the research questions can be formulated in a more specific version to supplement the research objectives.

Qualities of a Good Research Question

A research question must be:

i) Feasible, meaning it should be within the achievable scope in respects to the resources available.

ii) Clear, it should not be ambiguous thus it should consistently have the same meaning to anybody who reads it.

iii) Significant, it means that if the study answers the research questions, it will contribute some knowledge in the field of the study.

iv) Ethical; research questions should not infringe the do's and don'ts of a given group of people or professionals.

Conceptualized Variables and the Research Questions

The basis of a good conceptualization of the variables in a study is the literature review. Conceptualization involves a central idea or concept and other concepts relate to the idea and through this a research problem is born. Questions have the virtue of posing problems directly and satisfactorily without losing sight on the ultimate desirability and necessity of doing the research. A problem statement is a specific state focusing on the phenomenon that the researcher desires to describe, predict or explain and this statement can be expressed in question form, which requires a definite answer. The question must inquire into the relation between two or more variables and it should be presented in such away that the conclusion may be verifiable by empirical testing.

For example, after the researcher has described the phenomenon through examination of its symptoms, a number of questions can be raised by the researcher like:

i) Which motivational factors affect employee performance in the cement manufacturing firms in Kenya?

ii) To what extent does the identified motivational factors influence employee performance?

iii) Which organizational factors influence the relationship between the motivational factors and employee performance?

iv) What is the nature of relationship between the motivational factors and employee performance?

This study seeks to answer these questions by investigating the effect of motivation and employee performance in the cement manufacturing firms in Kenya. Once the problem is stated in this way, the researcher can formulate hypothesis to solve the problem. The researcher can summarize the variables and their postulated relationships in the conceptual framework, to aid better and quick understanding of the research problem.

The Research Questions Construction of Questionnaire and Questionnaire Items

The formulation of questions in the questionnaire is guided by the research questions where each research question forms a title in the questionnaire and a number of items are identified that can be examined in answering the research question. The researcher will then formulate questions on the itemized issues or aspects to be contained in the questionnaire.

For example, using the first research question in the hypothetical study given;

Which motivational factors affect employee performance in the cement manufacturing firms in Kenya?

Which motivational factors affect employee performance in the cement manufacturing firms in Kenya?

- a) Working conditions ☐
- b) Job security ☐
- c) Employee promotion ☐
- d) Employee remuneration ☐
- e) Manner of supervision ☐
- f) Employee recognition ☐

g) Others (Specify) *(i)* .... *(ii)* .... *(iii)* ....

Motivational Factors	5 Excellent	4 Very Good	3 Good	2 Fair	1 Poor
(a) Working conditions					
(b) Job security					
(c) Employee promotion					
(d) Employee remuneration					
(e) Manner of supervision					
(f) Employee recognition					
Others (Specify) (i) (ii) (iii)					

3. Does your organization have relevant policies guiding implementation of specific motivational issues?

Yes ☐ Not sure ☐ No ☐

Many more questions can be formulated from that first research question and when they are answered by the respondents, data analyzed, presented and interpreted appropriately then the problem under investigation can be addressed.

The Conceptual Framework, Research Questions, Research Objectives and Research Hypotheses

This section presents conceptualized study variables, generated research questions from the study variables, objectives of the researcher intends to achieve and presumed hypothetical relationships between the study variables.

The Effect of Risk Underwriting Decisions on the Performance of Insurance Firms in Kenya.

Fig. 9.1: Risk Underwriting Decisions and Organizational Performance

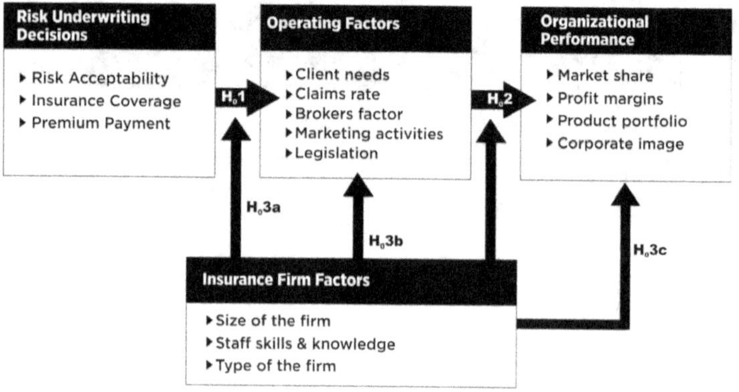

Source: Mudaki (2013)

Conceptually, the study seeks to examine the effect of risk underwriting decisions on the organizational performance. Risk underwriting decisions involves; risk acceptability, insurance coverage and premium payment, while organizational finance will be measured through market share, profit margins, product portfolio and corporate image. The relationship between the independent and dependent variables is intervened by operational factors which are; client needs, claims rate, brokers' factor, marketing activities and legislation. The relationship is also moderated by insurance farm factor like size of the firm, staff skill and knowledge and the type of firm.

Research Questions

The study seeks to answer the following questions;

i) What is the effect of risk underwriting decisions on the organizational performance?

ii) What is the influence of risk underwriting decisions on the insurance firms' operational factors?

iii) Does the operational factor of insurance firms affect their performance?

iv) Does the insurance firms' factor influence the relationship between risk underwriting decisions and organizational performance?

v) What is the effect of insurance firms' factors on the operating factors of insurance firms?

vi) Does an insurance firm factor influence organizational performance?

Research Objectives

The study seeks

i) To investigate the effect of risk underwriting decision on the organizational performance.

ii) To determine the influence of risk underwriting decisions on the insurance firms operational factors.

iii) To examine the effect of operational factor of insurance firms on their performance.

iv) To assess the influence of insurance firm factors on the relationship between risk underwriting decisions and the organizational performance.

v) To determine the effect of insurance firms' factors on the operating factors of the insurance firms.

vi) To examine the influence of insurance firm factors on the performance of insurance firms.

Chapter Ten

THE CONCEPTUAL FRAMEWORK AND LITERATURE REVIEW

Abstract

Literature review involves going through the existing empirical studies and other documented literature in an area of interest to the researcher. It enables the researcher to gather information in that area as presented by others but more importantly to identify the existing gaps that a particular study can fill. The constructs of a variable as presented in the conceptual framework guides the various sections of literature review in a research proposal, project or thesis. This makes the study be within the desired delimitation as designed by the researcher.

Key Words

Conceptual Framework and Literature Review.

Introduction

This chapter contains, meaning of literature review, rationale of literature review as well as the relationship between the conceptual framework and literature review.

Meaning of Literature Review

Literature review is an inevitable part of research which helps the researchers to identify the issues that establishes information about a particular research problem. Literature review is defined as the process of going through the documented literature in the area of your interest by other experts on the same area of study.

Researcher can summarizes the issues in a study area through construction of a conceptual framework. This will be helpful for the researcher to built and refine the research problem and objectives. It is against this background that in many studies, the conceptual framework is placed at the end of the literature review section in a study. Literature review helps the researcher to develop critical review and identify the research gaps on the area that needs to be addressed

Rational of Literature Review

Review of the literature helps the researcher in a number of ways namely:

i) It helps the researcher in building a case for the study in the background of the study. The symptoms to the research problem are shown.

ii) Also it helps the research to know the scope of previous studies in relation to the phenomenon under investigation. The researcher will be able to know the aspects of the issue the others had addressed and whether they were comprehensively researched.

iii) A good statement of the research problem can only be stated by way of reviewed literature. The gap can be identified accordingly through thorough review of the literature.

iv) The construction of a conceptual framework comes after literature review. This is where the researcher conceptualizes the variables and their presumed relationship. The researcher presents a version of his understand of the phenomenon in a diagrammatical form, known as the conceptual framework.

v) Through the literature review a researcher is able to appreciate the work of others. The researcher will be at a better position to assess quality of different pieces of work in his areas of interest.

vi) An assessment can also be done on the research design used, target population, sample size and sampling procedure, research instruments and analysis of data, in the literature review. This will be useful in determine where appropriate research design was used, data collection instruments chosen and if the sample size was a good representative of the target population.

Relationship Between the Conceptual Framework and Literature Review

After a researcher has constructed the conceptual framework the specific sub-sections on the literature review chapter can be guided by the conceptual framework variables. The use of the conceptual framework in guiding the specific sections in the literature review chapter is necessary because it helps the researcher to remain focused on the gap the study would like to fill. For example, in a study titled; "Income Generating Activities and Financing of the Public in Kenya".

By using the conceptual framework in figure 7.1 to guide the development of the literature review section of this hypothetical study, the following sub-sections are suitable;

2.1 Introduction

This chapter describes the overview of income generating activities in the public universities in developed countries in Africa, in East African and in Kenya. It also presents the types of income generating activities in the Kenyan public universities, their strategic management, income generated from these activities and employment opportunities they provide. The chapter finally examines the relationship between income generating activities and financing of the public universities in Kenya.

2.2 An Overview of Income Generating Activities

- Defining income generating activities.
- Purpose of income generating activities.
- Give an account of how the public universities in the developed countries establish, and manage their income generating activities.
- Examine the amount of income generated by these activities in those countries.
- Give the same account of how the public universities in Africa, East African and Kenya establish, manage and amount of income generated.

2.3 Income Generating Activities Tenet

The income generating activities can be examined through the valuation of the four tenets as expressed through; types of income generating activities, strategic management of the income generating activities, proportion of income they inject in the budget of the public universities and job opportunities provided by the income generating activities.

2.3.1 Types of Income Generating Activities in the Kenyan Public Universities

- Examine them in two categories, that is, product oriented activities and service oriented activities.
- Detail the challenges involved in both the orientations and compare the type of orientation which is most preferred and why.
- Compare the income generated by each type.

2.3.2 Strategic Management of the Income Generating Activities

- Compare and contrast the management of these activities

with those in the corporate world, bench mark with the best practices among the leading organizations.

- Explore whether or not the management approach adopted, explain the performance of these income generating activities.

2.3.3 Proportion of Income Injected by the Income Generating Activities in the Budget of the Public Universities.

- Examine the performance of these income generating activities in terms of; profit margins, efficiency levels, sales turnover and number of branches.
- Assess identifiable projects, like laboratories, lecture theaters, hostels, learning and teaching materials, street lighting, catering unit foodstuff subsidized by output or income from the income generating activities.
- Examine the consolidated annual account and reports of the public universities sources of income. Determine the proportion of income contributed by the income generating activities expressed as a percentage of the total income. Analyses this for a period of (5–10) years or over.
- Also in examining their performance in term of matching the income generated with the expenses incurred to generate such income, be keen on expenses like wages and salaries, cost of the raw materials among other operational costs.

2.3.4 Employment Opportunities Provided by the Income Generating Activities

- Like any other enterprise, the income generating activities are expected to contribute to the industrial observation rates thus the researcher should explore the number of people engaged in these activities.

- Also look at the work-study programme they support to the needy students.
- The researcher should also be keen on examining the size of the enterprise with the number of people employed.

2.4 University Factors

The university factors are characterized by the age of the institution, tone at the top (control environment) and university location.

- In analyzing these factors, the researcher can simply examine them in paragraph form, that is, each factor can take between four to five paragraphs depending on the information available and how critical the factor is presumed in moderating the relationship between the income generating activities and financing of public universities.
- Another approach that can be adopted in the examination of the university factors is giving them sub-titles. For example, 2.4.1 can take age of the institution; 2.4.2 can take tone at the top and 2.4.3 to take university location.
- In either approach, the researcher is expected to look at how these factors are presumed to be either enhancing or negating the relationship between income generating activities tenet. For example, the infant universities and university colleges may be suffering from weak financial framework to attract and retain highly qualified and experienced personnel in the income generating activities they may be running. However, in the case of the public universities that have been in existence for a longer period of time they might have accumulated the financial resources for the effective operations of their enterprises.

- The tone at the top usually determines the way organizations are managed. For example; management overrides on the established policies by the top level management. These may comprise best management practices, internal control systems and a sense of commitments on the firms' practices, organization culture and values. It may also enhance the best practices.
- On the university location, the researcher is expected to examine the rural established set up and the urban located universities.
- The researcher should analyse the advantages and disadvantages of either site in terms of the type of income generating activities, customer target for the product produced and services offered, competition by other players in the market which may determine the market share, profit margin and sales revenue over a given period of time.

2.5 Financing of the Public Universities

- Examine the exchequer funding of the public universities.
- Increased operational costs of the public universities due to number of students admitted. This leads to demand for more funds.
- Explore the demand for infrastructural facilities like hostels, laboratories and lecture theaters which necessitates more funding.
- Need for term loans like bonds for development of public universities to be explored.
- Privately sponsored students programmes (PSSP) should also be examined as a source of finance to the universities.

2.6 Relationship Between Income Generating Activities and Financing of the Public Universities

- This is the critical review of literature where the gaps are shown and how the study bridge the gaps.
- The symptoms observed in the tenets of income generating activities are consolidated and their presumed influence on the dependent variable; financing of public universities is examined.
- The manipulation of the income generating activities tenets will be manifested through profit margins, efficiency levels and other indicators.

2.7 The Conceptual Framework

This study is guided by the conceptual framework in figure 10.1

Fig. 10.1 Income Generating Activities and Financing of the Public Universities

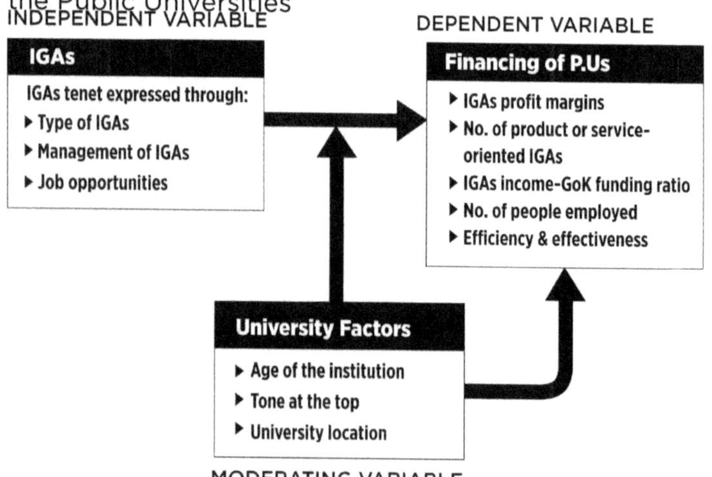

Source: Self conceptualization (2019)

The study is based on the premises that IGAs contribute in the financing of the public universities but this relationship is moderated by a number of university factors like age of the institution, tone at the top and university location.

Table 10.1: Shows a Summary of how the Literature Review Section can Look Like Through the Guidance of the Conceptual Framework

CHAPTER TWO

LITERATURE REVIEW

2.1   Introduction

2.2   An Overview of Income Generating Activities

2.3   Income Generating Activities Tenet

     2.3.1 Types of Income Generating Activities in the Public Universities

     2.3.2 Strategic Management of the Income Generating Activities

     2.3.3 Proportion of Income Injected by the Income Generating Activities in the Budget of the Public Universities

     2.3.4 Employment Opportunities Provided by Income Generating Activities

2.4   University Factors

2.5   Financing of the Public Universities

2.6   Relationship Between Income Generating Activities and Financing of the Public Universities.

2.7   The Conceptual Framework of Income Generating Activities and Financing of the Public Universities.

BIBLIOGRAPHY

Anderson, J. Duston, B.H and **Pool** M. (1990). *Thesis and Assignment Writing.* New Delhi: Wiley Eastern Limited

Adams, G. and **Schvaneldt**. (1985). *Understanding Research Methods.* New York: Longman Inc.

Babbie, E. (1992). *The Practice of Social Research.* California: Wadswork Publishing Company.

Best, J and **Khn** J. (2002). *Research Methods.* New Delhi: New Age International Design Limited.

Campdell, W.G and **Ballous**, S.U. (1990). *Form and style, Thesis, Report,* Term Papers. Eighth Edition. Boston: Houghton Milflin Company.

Cohen et al (2000). *Research Methods in Education.* Fifth Edition: London.

Cooper, D.R and **Schindler**, P.S. (2003). *Business Research Methods.* Eighth Edition. New Delhi: Tala McGraw Hill.

Dooley, D. (2004). *Social Research Methods.* New Delhi: Prentice Hall

Frederic J. G and **Lori-Ann**, B.F. (2006). *Research Methods for the Behavioural Sciences.* Second Edition. USA: Thomson Wadasworth.

Gitau, A.N. (2013) *Qualitative Research Methods.* Nairobi: Kijabe Press Publishers

Ghauri, P. and **Kell**, G. (2010). *Research Methods in Business Studies*. Fourth Edition. England: Prentice Hall.

Hart, C. (2005). *Doing Literature Review*. New Delhi: Sage Publications Limited.

Isaark, S and **Michael**, W.S. (1971). *Handbook in Research and Evaluation*. San Diego California: Edits Publishers

Kasente, D.H. (1995). *Processes Influencing Gender Differences in Access to Post Secondary Institutions in Uganda*. Nairobi: Academy Science Publishers

Kasomo, D. (2007). *Research Methods in Humanities and Education*. Eldoret: Zapf Chencery.

Kerlinger, F.N. (1973). Foundations of Behavioral Research Second Edition. New Delhi: Subject Publication

Kerlinger, F.N. (1983). *Foundations of Behavioral Research* First Edition. New Delhi: Subject Publication

Kombo, D.K and **Tromp**, D.L. (2006). *Proposal and Thesis Writing- An Introduction*. Nairobi: Pauline Publications

Kothari, C.R. (2003). *Research Meth+odology, Methods and Techniques*. New Delhi: Wishwa Prakshan

Lucey, T. (2000). *Quantitative Technique: An Instructional Manual*. London: Oxford University Press.

Malhotra, N.K. (2007). *Marketing Research. An Applied Orientation* (5th Edition). New Delhi: Prentice Hall of Indian Private Limited.

Mudaki, F. (2013) *Risk Underwriting Decisions and Insurance Firms; Performance In Kenya*. Masters Thesis: Mmust, Kenya

Mugenda, O.M. **Mugenda**, A.G. (1999). *Research Methods, Quantitative and Qualitative Approaches*, Nairobi: African Centre for Technology Studies (ACTS) Press

Mwangi, N. (2009). *Fundamentals of Management Research Methods*. Nairobi: Macmillan Kenya Limited

Nsubuga, E.N.K. (2000). *Fundamentals of Educational Research*. Kampala: MK publishers.

O'Leary, Z. (2007). *The Essential Guide to Doing Research*. Seventh Edition. New Delhi: Vistraar Publication.

Oso, W.Y and **Onen**, D. (2005). A *General Guide To Writing Research Proposal and Report*. Kisumu: Option Press and Publishing.

Pauneerselvam, R. (2011). *Research Methods*. New Delhi: PHI Learning Private Limited.

Polonsky M. T. and **Waller**. D. (2005). *Designing and Managing a Research Project*. New Delhi: Sage Publications.

Pugh D. and **Phillips**, E.M. (1984). How to Get a PhD: *A Handbook for Students and Supervisors*. Second Edition. Buckingham: Open University

Sakaran, U (1992). *Research Methods for Business*. New York: John Wiley and Sons Inc.

Saunders, M. **Lewis** P. and **Thornhill** (2009). *Research Methods for Business Students*. Fifth Edition. England: Pearson's Education Limited.

Sounders, M. and **Thornhill**, A. (2007). *Research Methods for Business Students.* Rome: Pearson's Education Limited

Thou, J., **K'Ohonyo**, P.. **Kibera**, F. and **Wainaina**, G. (2011), *Customer Relationship Marketing and Competitiveness of Commercial Banks In Kenya*, Ph.D Thesis, UoN, Kenya

www.ingramcontent.com/pod-product-compliance
Lightning Source LLC
Chambersburg PA
CBHW070529160726
48003CB00004B/1740